MW01617005

Praise for
Smart Conversations

"As someone who's worked at the intersection of finance and innovation for over two decades, I can say this with confidence: *Smart Conversations* gets it. It turns generative AI into a practical engine for scalable, intelligent go-to-market execution."

—Aaron Harris
Global CTO at Sage

"Every marketer I know is trying to figure out how to rethink their playbook with Gen AI. Ian takes his proven methodology and shows, prompt-by-prompt, how to create and leverage customer micro verticals. This is the Gen AI playbook on how to create superior B2B marketing at scale."

—Martina Lauchengco,
Partner at Costanoa Ventures and Author of
LOVED: How to Rethink Marketing Tech Products

"In the tradition of *Crossing the Chasm*, this book helps you do something even harder: build intelligent, trust-based markets from scratch. It's not just about technology—it's about timing, tone, and transformation."

—Stuart Evans, PhD
Distinguished Service Professor at
Carnegie Mellon University Silicon Valley

"This book translates the promise of generative AI into actionable go-to-market strategies. As a CMO building in the AI space, I found it refreshingly practical and deeply aligned with how real conversations drive category growth."

—**Michelle Denogean**
CMO at Mindtrip and author of *GrowUp*

"I've worked with Ian on this strategy since 2016. What started as a smart idea became a full go-to-market system—now fueled by Gen AI. If you sell through others, this book is your blueprint."

—**Peyton Burch, CPA**
Vice President Channel Sales at Sage

"At Google, we learned that scale without precision is noise. *Smart Conversations* brings that lesson into the Gen AI era, giving B2B marketers at all sizes of business a playbook for driving predictable, measurable, intelligent growth."

—**Harry Davies**
VP of Marketing Strategy & Effectiveness at Sage

DR. IAN HOWELLS

Foreword by Rob Reid

SMART
c o n v e r s a t i o n s

Revolutionizing
B2B Marketing
with the
Generative AI
Playbook

Smart Conversations:
Revolutionizing B2B Marketing with the Generative AI Playbook
Copyright © 2025 by Ian Howells

The book comprises learnings and content from Ian's eighteen-month period as CMO at Intacct before it was acquired by Sage in 2017. The book was written before the author resumed working for Sage in 2025. In all cases throughout the book, Sage is the company and Intacct or Sage Intacct is the product.

First hardback edition May 2025
Cover Design: Kay McConnaughey
Illustrations: Kay McConnaughey
Editor: Abigail Dengler

Published by Berry Powell Press
Glendora, California
www.berrypowellpress.com

ISBN: 978-1-957321-23-3 (Hardback)
Library of Congress Control Number: 2025909709

Contents

For Carla and my boys, Tom, Jamie, and Rory

Foreword

In the ever-evolving landscape of B2B marketing, the ability to connect with customers on a deeply personal level has become paramount. Generic campaigns and broad strategies can no longer capture attention or build lasting loyalty. Worse yet, they are inefficient and costly.

Smart Conversations: Revolutionizing B2B Marketing with the Generative AI Playbook is the culmination of Ian Howells' decades-long journey in the tech industry. Throughout his career, Ian has witnessed firsthand the transformative power of personalized micro-vertical marketing.

From his early days at Ingres, competing against industry giants like Oracle, to his pivotal roles at Documentum, Intacct, and Sage, Ian learned that success hinges on understanding and addressing the unique needs of each customer group. Having worked alongside Ian at Documentum and Intacct, I saw how he built a systematic business practice that propelled both companies forward. This book distills his hard-earned insights and proven strategies, now amplified by the revolutionary capabilities of generative AI—specifically, ChatGPT.

Generative AI presents an unprecedented opportunity to create highly targeted, data-driven business plans in a fraction of the time, reducing what once took months to mere days. It enables marketers to deliver personalization at a micro-vertical level, making it possible to dominate entire market segments swiftly and efficiently. Through *Smart Conversations*, Ian guides you through selecting your audience, creating hyper-personalized strategies, engaging customers on their terms, and achieving a formidable competitive edge.

Whether you are a seasoned marketer or an executive looking to future-proof your strategy, this book equips you with the tools and methodologies needed to thrive in AI-driven marketing. Ian's systematic approach, deep experience, and engaging style make him the perfect guide for this journey.

The insights and strategies shared here will empower you to revolutionize your approach to B2B marketing and lead the charge into this new terrain.

Let's explore how you can transform your business, elevate your marketing efforts, and achieve remarkable success in today's dynamic business environment.

—Rob Reid
Retired Chairman, Middle Market Solutions, Intacct

Introduction

In today's fast-paced business landscape, business-to-business (B2B) marketing rules are being rewritten. Generic campaigns and one-size-fits-all strategies are a thing of the past. Today, a company's success is determined by its ability to capture entire communities with precise marketing messages. This task is further complicated by the fact that the targeted communities are constantly in motion, thereby becoming a moving target.

My journey into this landscape began long before AI-driven campaigns and data-driven personalization became industry norms. I was born and educated in Britain in the 1980s. Growing up, I became fascinated by technology and set on one day becoming a Chief Technology Officer (CTO). I attended Cardiff University for my PhD in computing. My first position as a young engineer was at a database software company called Ingres, formed by three professors from UC Berkeley.

At the time, our biggest competitor was Oracle, another sales-driven software company led by Larry Ellison. Larry has become a legend and one of the most famous CEOs in tech history. But being a young and naive engineer at the time, I wasn't too worried. I was familiar with their product and felt confident that ours was superior.

My confidence turned out to be misguided. We competed against Oracle for a time, but in the end, they didn't just beat us; they crushed us. I was perplexed. We had an excellent product and some of the best software engineers in the world. Others in the industry also seemed to share an understanding that we had the superior product.

What went wrong? Colleagues at other companies often remarked, "Great software you guys developed there. It's a shame about the marketing." *What did they mean? What does marketing have to do with why we failed?* At that time, I had a negative and inaccurate perception of marketing. What I did as an engineer was measurable, tangible, and valuable. I thought marketing was just a bunch of buzzwords and flashy giveaways.

Over time, I understood what others had already realized: it didn't matter how excellent our product was if we were not intimately connecting to our customers and showing them we had the solution to their most pressing problems. Oracle, in contrast, positioned itself as the answer to the customer's most urgent issues. In other words, our message conveyed that "We're here, and we're great." Oracle's message proclaimed, "We understand *you*, and we have the solution to your most pressing need." Our generalized approach couldn't compete.

In the decades since then, this same principle has only become more true: each group of customers is different, and an effective strategy acknowledges and embraces this fact.

Each customer group has different priorities, speaks a unique language, participates in other communities, and takes cues from distinct authorities. It's widely known that the same business strategy used when targeting a Wall Street Firm will not be equally effective with a not-for-profit (NFP). An effective plan matches the terrain. In other words, successfully reaching a multitude of markets with your marketing requires specific personalization.

In 1993, I transitioned from Ingres to a content management software company called Documentum, where I moved from engineering to marketing. After Documentum, I served in several other Software as a Service (SaaS) marketing roles. I worked as the VP of Marketing with a company called SeeBeyond and as CMO of Alfresco, Argyle Data, and Intacct (before Sage acquired it), along with a handful of other positions. I then took a year to write this book before returning to my role at Sage as VP of Product Marketing in 2025.

I have spent the last three decades of my career creating a way for businesses to personalize effective strategies. At Intacct, I implemented a plan that significantly increased Annual Recurring Revenue (ARR) in four years and transformed the company's Go-to-Market (GTM) approach. I found the secret sauce.

Yet when I talk about personalization as the golden rule of B2B marketing, I can practically hear the heart rates of the sales and marketing teams thumping from stress. And I get it! I have created and reviewed hundreds of strategic marketing plans for over twenty years. They have an incredible impact when done well, but there is no escaping that the process is complex and laborious. We have long recognized that common strategies are not the most effective—but often, generic campaigns are all the available resources can cover.

Some teams venture into more targeted marketing with the wisdom to adapt their approach for various audience groups. But at the end of the day, a highly personalized strategy can take months to develop. And what if it doesn't take? This ideal isn't realistic for many teams' time, money, and workforce.

How does one achieve this level of precision and personalization at scale? Generative AI is a game-changing tool to transform our approach.

I believe generative AI is the most significant change in business strategy planning in the last twenty years. For years, AI has been able to perform tasks like data analysis and problem-solving, but the subset of generative AI takes performance to a new level. Rather than just analyzing data, it creates new content through text, music, and images.

Generative AI offers marketers an unprecedented opportunity: the ability to create highly targeted, data-driven marketing plans in a fraction of the time it once took. It can deliver personalization at a micro-vertical level in days rather than months. This is not just the future of marketing; it's the present, and those who embrace it will have a significant competitive edge.

How to Get the Most Out of This Book

I wrote this book for business owners, marketing and sales teams, and executives looking to future-proof their strategy. Some concepts may feel elementary to executives, but the truth is that even seasoned professionals make common mistakes. And even if they understand a concept, many executives struggle to explain it to their teams.

This book is also applicable to a variety of business types and sizes. If you are a smaller or medium-sized business, this method will teach you how to compete with slow bureaucratic giants and beat them. If you represent a large, established company, this method will allow you to use your resources more effectively to move in more nimble and dynamic ways.

In this book, you will find my battle-tested B2B marketing playbook—combined with the revolutionary tools of generative AI that make this approach accessible as never before. The first two chapters will outline the rationale behind the method. Chapters Three through Seven will move through the central strategy and how to build it for yourself. The final two chapters walk you through how to implement the plan and win the markets you set out for.

In this playbook, each chapter will conclude with what I call a "Smart Conversation" with ChatGPT. A Smart Conversation demonstrates a way of collaborating with this generative AI tool. I have chosen ChatGPT because I tried the method on multiple generative AI models, and OpenAI's model was the only one that could do what I asked. Other models told me how to do what I asked; ChatGPT did it for me.

Through these conversations, I will walk you through choosing an audience, creating a hyper-personalized strategy, connecting to your customer on their terms, and dominating entire market segments in twelve to eighteen months.

Lastly, before diving in, I encourage you to think of this book like a cookbook. As with a recipe, each step builds on the last in a specific order. I recommend moving sequentially. That said, if you need the method now and don't have time to read, go to page 203, where you will find the Conversation Library with all of the prompts so you can get started right away. This playbook will give you everything you need to thrive in the modern marketing era. Now, let's get started and discover how you can lead the charge into this new terrain.

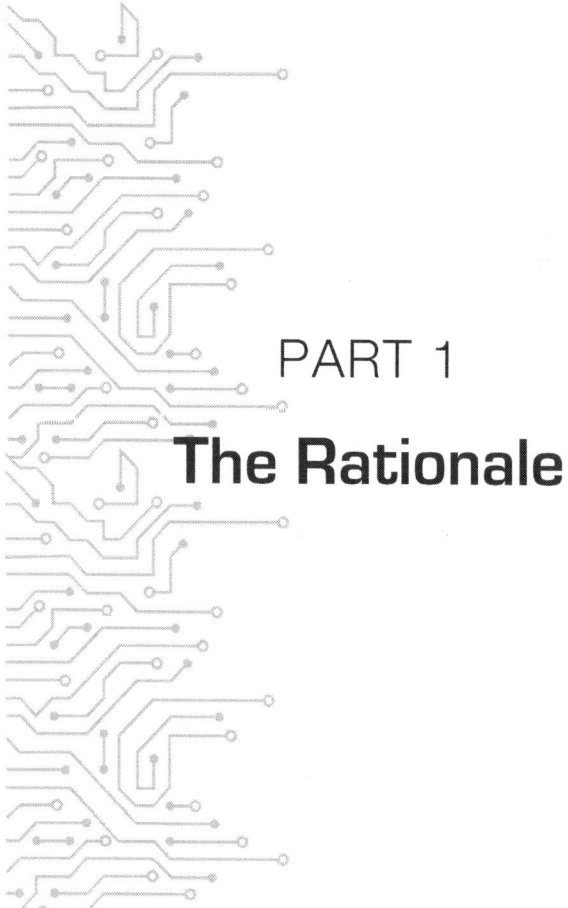

PART 1

The Rationale

CHAPTER 1
Make Markets, Not War

Marketers have long been forced to walk the tightrope between personalization and scale. On one hand, companies celebrate marketing campaigns that feel personal, timely, and human to their audience. These types of campaigns drive conversations and create loyal "fanbases." Yet these take significant resources to develop, and they often target relatively small sectors of an audience. Without reaching a critical mass of audience members, even the most bespoke campaigns fall short of their intended impact.

You need a personalized plan at the right level, but you also need *enough* plans to scale and cover every group you want to sell to. Only the most prominent companies can afford to have dedicated industry marketing staff to cover all these bases. The result is that most B2B companies compromise. They go to market with a horizontal, product-centric strategy and put forth broad campaigns that lack relevance or specificity.

Just as bad is the "Vertical Strategy." Beware of any company that puts "Industry" on the menu bar of their website with drop-down options for "Manufacturing" or "Financial Services." It's clear they are trying to find the balance between personalization and scale here: they are attempting to capture the business of multiple industries while tailoring the message uniquely to each. However, even after segmenting their audience by industry, those segments are still incredibly broad.

Do they believe that all companies—even in the same industry—have identical attributes and needs? By lumping all financial companies into a simplistic drop-down, they essentially say, "We believe USAA, Morgan Stanley, Wells Fargo, and the Dalio Family Office are all the same." That is not the case. For example, an investment bank, a retail bank, a regional bank, and a wealth management firm are incredibly different: They have unique buyers, drivers, and priorities. Investment banks want to provide their high-wealth clients with sophisticated financial instruments. Retail banks want to provide their regular clients with basic banking facilities and simpler financial instruments on a larger scale. Regional banks want to prioritize giving their clients a friendly, local feel to set themselves apart. A one-size-fits-all service for all financial companies will completely miss the nuance of each institution's needs.

What is needed is a way to get the best of both worlds. We need a way to personalize our plans to the tribe level—capturing a true group of businesses that speak the same language and move as one. We need to scale this to capture a large number of those groups.

The Marketer's War Room

We need a better strategy for this terrain. When I give presentations, this metaphor often helps: rather than looking at the market through the lens of a CMO, look at it through the lens of a military general examining the battle landscape. (If that feels too far off, imagine you are knee-deep in a video game or board game like Risk or Settlers of Catan.)

Think of your Total Addressable Market (TAM) as a series of hills on a map. Which might you conquer to expand your territory? You see:

- A hill that is very large but very heavily defended with machine guns on top
- A hill that is very large and poorly defended but covered by snow
- A hill that is medium-sized and poorly defended with similar medium-sized hills around it

THE BATTLE LANDSCAPE

As the general, what are your options?

Option 1: Go bold and attack all the hills at once. This strategy is a mile wide and an inch deep. Your team will be spread so thin that you're not likely to win any of the hills.

Option 2: Take on the biggest hill under the mantra of "high risk, high reward." This strategy is akin to World War I, when people came out of the trenches and ran into machine gun bullets. It almost always fails with heavy casualties.

Option 3: Go for the large hill covered by snow. After all, it's poorly defended! But unfortunately, you don't have the equipment (like snowshoes or cold-weather gear) to traverse through snow. You'd freeze to death if you tried. There's no way forward here.

Option 4: Attack the group of medium-sized hills. Any defenses they have are outdated and outmatched. The population is sick of the old guard anyway! They will welcome you in. Once you've conquered the first hill, the surrounding hills will fall quickly into line with no casualties.

The rationale behind these options is obvious to the general or the experienced player of Settlers of Catan. While the payoff of the more significant hills may be tantalizing, the pursuit is either too costly or unfeasible. Rather than ending at a loss, option #4 represents a genuine and substantial gain that, when combined, will amount to more land than one of the large hills anyway.

Now, place yourself back in an executive or marketing and sales team mindset. Suddenly, you will see that traditional marketing constantly pursues futile strategies.

Option 1: Attacking all the hills simultaneously, translated into marketing speak, is the horizontal product strategy. The rationale behind this is often that "the product is horizontal." After all, something like a mug or a computer keyboard is a product that many people across industries can use. In theory, you'll capture the largest TAM by attacking them all.

The reality is that by targeting everyone, you don't effectively reach anyone. Like the general, you waste resources by scattering them and being average everywhere rather than being effective in any market. You treat good customers (who are low cost to acquire and don't churn) the same as bad customers (who are expensive to gain, complain about the product functionality, and have a high churn rate). Ultimately, you lose to the larger, stronger companies or smaller, more focused attacks.

Option 2: Attacking the huge but heavily defended hills is the macho strategy of attacking the market leader's home territory. Greed motivates this attack as you imagine the bliss of a world without your primary competitor and where all their customers are yours.

However, this strategy is far more driven by ego than reality. If your competitor is the leader in this market, dethroning them will take ample resources, time, and funds you may not have. Their customers may not even be motivated to switch. Ultimately, there is a horrible win rate for this type of endeavor.

Option 3: Attacking the large, poorly defended hill covered by snow is akin to pursuing a rich market with great potential but where you have a poor product-market fit. Again, this strategy tends to be driven by greed, as the TAM seems enormous, and if they're tired of the old products they're using, they may be willing to switch. This market seems ripe for the taking, and perhaps it is—but not by you.

The reality of this strategy is that you don't have what this market needs. You have little knowledge of its nuances. To access this market, you must completely rework your product through a never-ending list of functionality requirements for a Minimum Viable Product (MVP). This strategy would take a ton of work and investment for you even to become a contender. Why waste all this investment when you already have a product that could be a perfect fit for someone else?

Option 4: Finally, we have the option of attacking the medium-sized, poorly defended hills with old, worn-out defenses. These hills are the slightly smaller markets that aren't as flashy—the ones that are often overlooked. They are dominated by legacy players: companies that have been in business for many years or even decades. They may be deeply rooted in the communities they serve and have a loyal customer base. You've likely never even heard of them; they've been around so long that they don't need to market their product. Their customers may very well have never had any other option.

However, these companies are vulnerable to being dethroned as customers grow sick of archaic systems that no longer meet their modern needs. It's also possible that the population cannot afford the cost of the legacy players gouging them because there is no alternative. It is also a market in which your core product is naturally a good fit, though you may not even be aware of it at first.

Do you see how valuable these hills can be if you find them? You can step in as the liberator, creating a market for the new way forward, bringing them into the present, and addressing needs that have been weighing on them unresolved for years, if not decades. Not only do you become their hero, but this whole group moves as one. Once one goes, all the others fall into line. If you crack this, you can dominate this segment and get a hugely dispropor-tionate win rate, fewer days to close, a bigger average deal size, and a network effect within the community.

This plan solves the tension between personalization and scale. Yes, you still need to personalize a plan for each hill. But because the adjacent hills are relatively similar, you don't have to start each plan from scratch. You only have to adapt it to the new hill's needs. And since they are all connected, winning the first hill will give you credibility with the next. The more you win, the more integrated you become in this network of related, ripe, and overlooked communities. You have won on personalization and scale without draining all your resources.

Most marketing strategies combine options one, two, and three, but option four is the best way forward.

The "Medium-Hills" Strategy in the Real World

An excellent example of this strategy in action is my time working at Documentum, a company started by John Newton. John had been my boss at Ingres, and though I was young in my career, he saw a spark in me. When Ingres folded, he gathered a team to start Documentum, where I became one of the first employees.

Documentum is a content management platform designed to manage very large documents, such as a 500,000-page pharmaceutical drug submission form or aircraft manuals. You need a special type of software to store and share these documents. Again, we were confident we had an excellently designed product that would provide a new, invaluable alternative to clunky legacy systems.

Make no mistake: the product was horizontal and could be used across various industries. However, John did not plan to repeat Ingres's missteps. We would not choose battle option #1 and take on all big document services, saying, "Documentum can manage bigger documents than our competitors." This time, we knew that was not a compelling enough message. It did not demonstrate any unique understanding of the client's needs.

We also didn't pursue option #2 and try to oust our major competitors. At the time, the two biggest products for editing massive documents like this were Frame and Interleaf. These were billion-dollar large-document specialists. We were still a relatively small business with twenty-something employees and less than ten million per year in revenue. So, we didn't try to create a new version of these or an extension to use within these programs. If we had directly tried to take their business, these more established companies would have blown us out of the water.

In this new company, John understood the customer and the forces shaping their business. This time, he knew building an excellent product meant nothing if the customers he built it for couldn't get value from it.

We had very few employees, but John prioritized bringing on strong marketing leaders. He brought on people like Robert Reid as the VP of Marketing. Rob is an enterprise software serial CEO from companies including Zenith, UpShot, Oracle, and later Intacct, and he is a successful board member. CEO and ex-Intel Marketing exec Jeff Miller led the team. We also hired business strategist Geoffrey Moore to consult with us before he penned his famous books *Crossing the Chasm* and *Inside the Tornado*. We did not know then that we were the guinea pigs for his new approach and Go-to-Market strategy. We all got religion about the process that Geoffrey Moore taught us.

Following this approach, we carried out in-depth prospect interviews to understand the Ideal Customer Profile (ICP). Two industries we paid special attention to were pharmaceutical research and development (R&D) companies and commercial insurance companies, knowing both had massive documents to manage.

However, in our research, we noticed that while commercial insurance companies were a good market, our product didn't already have everything they needed—much like in battle option #3. These companies dealt with highly complex commercial insurance claims, and there were a myriad of rules around these claims that were different in every state. Adapting our product to fit these needs would have been an enormous undertaking.

On the other hand, when we looked at the pharmaceutical R&D market, we noticed via interviews that dozens of companies within were affected by a considerable shift. Using Moore's terminology, these companies were experiencing a "discontinuity": an industry shift so substantial that they literally could not continue operating as they had been.

The shift was that their "blockbuster drugs" winnings were drying up. Think of a blockbuster movie. Certain drugs become so popular that they keep the whole company afloat (in the modern day, Ozempic may be a good example). But after a while, even the smashers stop selling, and that's what was happening here. These companies needed to find the next megahit and reduce the time it took to file and process new global drug applications. Otherwise, they'd risk getting bought out by another pharma company.

Like in option #4, Documentum's product was a perfect match for this group of hills tired of the old guard and urgently ready to switch over at once. Documentum delivered: We reduced the time it took to process a global New Drug Application (NDA) from eighteen months to six weeks and generated an additional one million dollars per day. We were officially the heroes.

In eighteen months, Documentum became the new standard for nearly all the major pharma R&D companies. Eventually, even the FDA started accepting NDAs directly into Documentum. That was a major pivot and success that proved Moore's strategy effective. We quickly went from a new player to a dominant force.

The underlying strategy in this example is what I have now been continually building upon and refining for over twenty years. Not to mention, this was all before the introduction of generative AI. That is to say, even more is possible now. And not only is it possible, but it is also cost-effective, reproducible, and achievable at an even higher scale.

The rest of this book is about discovering "medium-hills" markets like these. It works whether you are trying to access new industries or win over more customers in a single sector. You'll learn how to become the hero and expand your company's impact without wasting resources *or* making a war you can't win.

CHAPTER 2
Micro-Vertical Marketing Made Easy

At this point, we need both personalization and scale. We have determined the most effective strategy to achieve both: pursuing the "medium-sized hills." If you are following me up to this point, the natural next questions to ask include:

- What exactly is a "medium-sized hill"?
- How do I find them?
- How do I know if they're good to attack?
- How do I know if I have what it takes to win these hills?
- Which one do I start with?
- How can I be sure they'll switch to me?
- Once I've chosen one, how do I create my strategy plan?
- How can generative AI help me with all this?

This chapter will define "medium-sized hills" more specifically. The following chapters will help you answer these other questions through a strategic business plan.

Introducing Micro-Vertical Marketing

A single medium-sized hill, as translated from the hills analogy into marketing, is otherwise known as a micro-vertical. Micro-vertical marketing is a strategy that focuses on targeting very niche segments within a larger industry.

A simple definition of a micro-vertical is a grouping of companies or firms that are insiders to one another. They are defined and recognized internally and externally. Characteristics of these companies or firms include:

- They are very similar to one another
- They have the same needs
- They have resemblant buyers who identify themselves in the same way
- Their buyers share roughly the same business problems
- They network and communicate with each other
- They meet at associations or conferences to share experiences among close colleagues
- They have rankings where industry metrics drive the ordering

For example, a vertical market might be manufacturing, but a micro-vertical market would be children's toy manufacturing. Manufacturing is a vast category that can include airplane manufacturing (Boeing), auto manufacturing (General Motors), toy manufacturing (Mattel), pharmaceutical manufacturing (Pfizer), or a million other types of manufacturing, from dishwashers to pens. Targeting manufacturing is pointless; you try to be everything to everybody, but ultimately, you become nothing to anyone. However, choosing a much narrower segment, like children's toy manufacturing, gives you a concrete and somewhat unified audience to aim for.

How do you know if a micro-vertical is good for you to target? We'll get into more detail later, but the simple answer is this: a *viable* micro-vertical for your team needs what you have to offer, is big enough to be of interest to you, and is small enough for you to dominate not just one company but a whole portfolio of them simultaneously.

Micro-Vertical Marketing: Manual Versus Generative AI

To dominate a micro-vertical, you need a good plan. After twenty years working with these plans, I can attest that the results are excellent when done well. But there is no getting away from the fact that the process is laborious for the following reasons and more:

- Industry experts are not always good at learning new micro-verticals and creating the necessary material for a sales team playbook.

- It is hard to find great product marketing people with the right skillset and curiosity to learn about a new micro-vertical and then create the necessary material for a sales team playbook (there are great people out there, but not enough to go around).

- There is an art to finding a micro-vertical segment at the right level and creating an attack plan for not just one but a series of segments (hills).

- After months of planning, people don't want to admit that the market they've been pursuing isn't a fit, so they often go ahead with plans that are doomed from the start.

How does generative AI play into this equation? Gen AI is the solution to each of these obstacles and more.

The Generative AI Journey

Generative AI is the maximal, most widespread shift since the Internet, and over time, it may prove to be even bigger. Its emergence reminds me of when the Internet first arrived.

With the advent of the Internet, many vendors copied their client-server applications into a browser. They looked awful, with cluttered and unresponsive layouts not built for a smaller screen. That's because they were designed for an old system; they were not adapted to fit and use the newest technology. Web-native companies overtook these vendors, delivering applications using all the power of the Internet.

A similar thing happened with the introduction of the mobile browser. Many businesses with websites thought the website's mobile version would translate simply to a handheld device. It became quickly apparent that was not the case. At some point, we have all experienced the frustration of trying to access a website on our phones when the website was not designed for a seamless mobile experience. Full-screen web applications didn't translate to the browser on a mobile device. The App Store and other creators who designed websites for a mobile-first approach used the full power of what the smartphone had to offer, and they quickly dominated their competitors.

The same evolution is happening with generative AI, which will forever change business strategy planning. Those who embrace it only in part, copying and pasting old strategies into the new framework while missing its true potential, will be left behind.

I started my journey with generative AI in 2023 when I attended a course called "ChatGPT Prompt Engineering for Developers." The legendary Andrew Ng and Isa Fulford from OpenAI delivered it. My mind went into overdrive about the potential to apply it to micro-vertical business planning. I got my research hat on and read everything I could on ChatGPT, prompt engineering, and other generative AI tools. I wanted to become an expert on applying generative AI to B2B micro-vertical marketing, so I took a year off to research it and write this book. Since the course I took centered around ChatGPT, which is currently regarded as the best AI chatbot, that is the model I chose to work with.

As I began experimenting with the power of ChatGPT for marketing, I found myself underutilizing it at first. Initially, I used it like a super search engine, asking it questions and having it summarize the answers. This usage was already saving me time—I was impressed. However, like the pre-Internet and pre-mobile companies, I was still ultimately using my old ways. ChatGPT was helping me execute my old strategies more easily.

As I grew into a more "intermediate" user of ChatGPT, I realized I could use it to automate laborious parts of my planning process. For example, I mentioned how many interviews we conducted when setting the strategy for each company I worked at. I would string a series of wooden desks in a line and spread countless customer interview documents along the desks, looking for commonalities. That would take me hours and days, at least. With ChatGPT, I could upload fifty customer interviews, and within a few minutes, it could consolidate multiple sources of information and identify concise lists of themes and commonalities for me.

While that was a more effective use of the technology, I still relied on the basic methods I was comfortable with, which had helped me build a successful career over the years. I was still thinking through a pre-GPT mindset and missing out on the technology's full potential.

However, writing this book radically changed my perspective on and understanding of Gen AI technology . I began to ask myself: What is this really capable of? What might I ask this technology if I shed my preconceptions—or if I'd grown up with this technology and had no preconceived limitations of what it could or couldn't help me with?

The mindset I have adopted and must work to embrace is that of a "Gen AI-native." That is, to ask the questions I listed above: How would someone who grew up with this technology as second nature use it?

The Harvard Business Review conducted a study on how people are actually using this technology to solve problems in their personal and professional lives. (This study also centered on ChatGPT.) Here are just a few samples from this research, published in the article "How People Are Really Using Gen AI":

"I love it for brainstorming because it's like the perfect teammate. It can keep up with me and doesn't get hung up on dead-end ideas, and it can summarize what we come up with so it's easier to present or reference later on."

"I have to write a lot of .vb and Excel formulas to reconcile data from less technical people. ChatGPT helps 45-minute tasks take about three to five minutes."

"A car wash damaged my wife's SUV and refused to pay, so GPT drafted a demand letter for me, and I took them to small claims court."

"I use it to check my own biases with op-eds and speeches and other political stuff. If something makes me feel strongly, I copy it into ChatGPT and ask it to tell me the logical fallacies and possible misinformation in the piece. It is a HUGE gut check!!"

"There was a particular cookie my grandmother used to give me and I really liked the taste and texture, and I had looked at the grocery to no avail until one evening ... I decided that it might be fruitful to ask ChatGPT for help ... It was SnackWell's."

While some respondents claimed Gen AI was too error-prone and unuseful in their lives, the anecdotal evidence is so widespread that it has become clear there is hardly an aspect of our modern lives that Gen AI cannot be of help with. There is no getting away from it.

Learning to collaborate with generative AI is truly a journey. Think of learning ChatGPT for B2B marketing as learning a new language. If any of you have ever been to Paris and gotten in a taxi, you will know that the more fluent you are in French, the less abuse you will get from the taxi driver! We start learning a language by directly translating what we know into this new form, but a direct translation is clunky at best—nonsensical or offensive at worst. As we become fluent, we stop mentally translating each word through the lens of English and start thinking French first. That is the standard of mastery for language and generative AI: releasing our preconceptions and using this language as if we had grown up with it.

If you are in B2B marketing or sales, not using generative AI in 2025 is like saying in 2005, "I'm a bit old school; I don't use the Internet." Don't be that dinosaur. Start getting the personalization and scale you need to compete on a personal and business level.

Thinking Gen AI-First

I often see people searching for the "magic prompts" when learning to use Gen AI. For example, I see people asking ChatGPT, "Write me a marketing plan," or books boasting of "100 prompts to make you a ChatGPT millionaire." As with every new market, there is a lot of BS.

ChatGPT natives understand that unlocking the technology's potential is not about finding the magic prompt. Don't get me wrong: there is an art to prompt engineering, which you will learn in this book. But what truly unlocks the technology is not a particular prompt. Instead, it is about understanding ChatGPT as a true collaborator.

For example, I could ask ChatGPT:

- *Create a playlist of ten songs for me*

This is like asking it to "create a marketing plan for me." It will produce what you have requested, but the output will be as broad, generic, and unhelpful as the input.

It seems obvious, but it comes back to what Isa Fulford said in the course about being as specific as possible. Task the machine with something you need help with. Again, ask it as if it is a true collaborator who can handle the nuance of your plans.

I would get a very different response by asking:

- *Create me a playlist of ten songs*
- *From the 1980s and 1990s*
- *For a Valentine's Day meal*
- *Where I'm going to propose to my girlfriend*
- *During the last song*

Now you're cooking with gas!

When it responds, you might ask:

17

- *Can you replace any song released after 2010 with something more classic?*
- *Can you adjust the list so the playlist lasts under thirty minutes?*

The prompts are significant. But what's more important is that talking with ChatGPT is a conversation, not a diatribe. Therefore, we must mature from *"prompt engineering"* to *"conversation engineering."* We have to approach Gen AI as if we are engaging with an expert who has the collective brain power and expertise to give advice.

Consider ChatGPT a collection of all your best, most knowledgeable customers and partners in one room. Think of it as a Customer Advisory Board (CAB) you can ask advice and questions of 24/7, 365. Imagine your plan as dynamic, constantly being updated by the latest advice and intelligence filtered by you.

> We have to approach Gen AI as if we are engaging with an expert who has the collective brain power and expertise to give advice

If you were sitting in a room with all your best customers and advisors, you probably wouldn't think, "What is the best prompt to ask them?" or "How can I cram as many questions as possible into one sentence?" That's not how a conversation generally flows. You would likely want an interactive exchange to pick the collective brain.

That is what I call a "Smart Conversation," an exchange in which the user treats Gen AI as a collaborator and engineers interactive conversations to reach their goals in a fraction of the time it once took to do so.

Why I'm Using ChatGPT

One caveat: I cannot currently recommend that all generative AI models be used in this way. While writing this book, I tried my method on multiple models, and ChatGPT is the only one that can accomplish the task. Other models will *tell me* how to do what I am asking; ChatGPT will *do it*. Perhaps by the time you're reading this, other models can be used to conduct Smart Conversations, but for the sake of this book, we will focus on Smart Conversations with ChatGPT.

Principles of Smart Conversations

At a high level, these are the principles for conducting Smart Conversations:

- **Give ChatGPT a persona.** Always start by defining the role of the ChatGPT persona that will answer your B2B business strategy planning questions. For example, you might start the conversation by saying, "You are an expert on the Asset Management space and have been for over twenty years as a Chief Financial Officer and more lately as a Chief Investment Officer for a niche, high-growth asset manager."
- **Be specific.** Be as precise as possible about the question or task. For example, "I need to create an Ideal Customer Profile based on the attached customer case studies."
- **Ask one question at a time.** Ask a series of short, precise questions, and you will get much better answers than one prompt with many questions.
- **Input customer data.** Load up as much publicly available customer persona, industry data, or other relevant data as possible. It can be in PDF, Word, or CSV documents, etc. ChatGPT can intake and analyze more than just

words. Its analysis of spreadsheets is equally as powerful. GPTs support up to twenty documents.

- **Utilize ChatGPT's workspace, which is called a "GPT."** Within the overall ChatGPT program, you can create multiple GPTs. Think of a GPT as a folder of documents around a specific subject within the ChatGPT program. A GPT can store up to twenty documents—ten files per upload—and be used to collaborate with others. For example, if you are doing financial analysis on a company, use the GPT to share financial documents, such as annual reports, with your team members.

- **Use ChatGPT's access to the Internet.** Explicitly ask ChatGPT to browse the web and find any public analyst reports, comparison sites, buyer guides, blogs, social posts, or other reference materials from third parties. You can also directly ask ChatGPT to provide a list of the third-party resources it has used in its answers.

- **Remember that ChatGPT has memory.** When using ChatGPT, remember that you can continue the conversation without reiterating information each time. For example, I regularly use it to check the standings in the Champions League, a league of the best soccer clubs in Europe. I can ask, "Who is the top team in the Champions League?" and receive real-time results. I can follow up with questions like, "Who do they play next?" rather than restating the team's name, and I can ask, "Who are the top eight teams?" without restating that I'm asking about the Champions League. Its memory provides the context.

- **Ask follow-up questions.** If you want more detail, continue the conversation. For example, "I have read the customer needs and pain points. Which ones are critical, must-do projects this year vs. next year?"

With these Gen AI-first principles, those with even basic marketing knowledge and limited resources can develop excellent, researched, and reasoned micro-vertical business plans in days.

ChatGPT & Data Privacy

With all this new opportunity, hesitancies may also arise. Some companies, especially major ones, may not be willing to trust ChatGPT in this way—especially when it comes to importing customer data. A primary fear is that ChatGPT will retain that customer data and incorporate it into its model's knowledge base so that another user could search, "Who is Sage's biggest customer?" or worse, find one's entire customer database with a simple search.

That is what I call a "Smart Conversation," an exchange in which the user treats Gen AI as a collaborator and engineers interactive conversations to reach their goals in a fraction of the time it once took to do so.

This paranoia is understandable. The development of this technology moves faster than the regulations needed to secure it. And its creators have not always been forthcoming or integrous in scraping nearly every source on the web to feed their creation.

While general caution is undoubtedly merited, the inputs used in this system are not risks for your company. Consider the following:

- The amount of data you would share with ChatGPT is minimal (Customer Name, Website, Industry).
- It's likely you're already sharing this nominal subset of data with other AI tools (such as 6Sense).
- ChatGPT encrypts data both in motion and at rest (in motion means when I am actively conversing with ChatGPT; at rest means when it's being stored in ChatGPT).
- In the ChatGPT model, a checkbox in Settings under Data Controls allows users to specifically request that ChatGPT *not* use their data to improve its model. (Turn off "Improve the model for everyone.")

- Even if you didn't check the box and did allow ChatGPT to train its model with your data, it still wouldn't enable external users to search for the data shared in your conversation.
- Users can delete a conversation; the GPT will store it for thirty days and then delete it permanently.
- For additional assurance, users can purchase the ChatGPT Teams or Enterprise versions. ChatGPT will not use inputs or outputs to train its model by default when using these products.

Check your company's policy on using generative AI, and if your company's security person wants more information, direct them to the following footnote.[1] Each person and company must do their research and use their discretion, especially as the models evolve. That said, the paranoia around sharing information with ChatGPT most often comes down to fear of the unknown rather than a concrete reality.

The paranoia many are experiencing toward Gen AI parallels people's initial unease about storing information in the cloud. When cloud technology emerged, people believed you could *never* store your sales pipeline in the cloud, or else someone could steal it. Salesforce was a main driver that completely changed people's minds. Salesforce spends billions a year on customer security, and people soon realized their data was far more secure in

---

[1] OpenAI's enterprise offerings supports several key security and compliance standards, including:

1. SOC 2 Type II – OpenAI's enterprise services comply with SOC 2 Type II, ensuring strong security, availability, and confidentiality controls.
2. ISO/IEC 27001, 27017, 27018 – These certifications demonstrate adherence to international standards for information security management, cloud security, and data protection.
3. GDPR (General Data Protection Regulation) – OpenAI provides controls and data-handling mechanisms that align with GDPR for European users.
4. HIPAA (Health Insurance Portability and Accountability Act) – Some enterprise deployments may offer HIPAA compliance for handling healthcare-related data.
5. SOC 3 – A publicly available report summarizing OpenAI's SOC 2 compliance.
6. FISMA (Federal Information Security Management Act) – OpenAI's services may be assessed for government-level security compliance.

their systems than in their own. Today, the norm is storing customer or accounting data in the cloud even for the most prominent and security-conscious organizations.

I believe the same evolution of trust is inevitable with generative AI. People will continue to use prudence, but sharing data with Gen AI will soon be seen as a part of business as usual—an essential part.

Back to the article in the Harvard Review, the review aptly concluded with the remark, "The 5% or whatever who use it effectively are going to smoke the others." The following chapters will show you how to use Gen AI to create a micro-vertical plan using a real-life scenario. I think you will quickly see how ChatGPT smokes the old way. And if you are willing to take the leap, this book will make you part of the 5%.

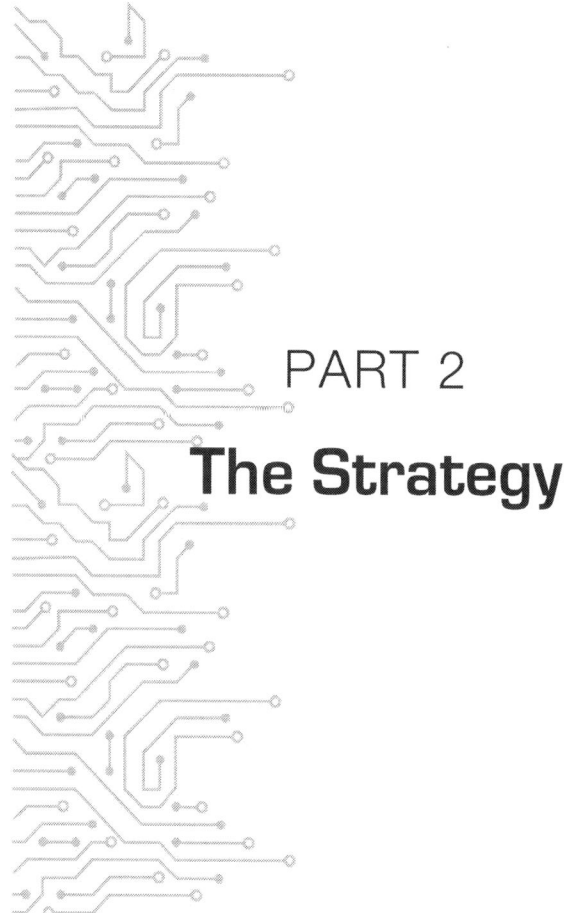

PART 2

The Strategy

CHAPTER 3
Finding Your Hidden Fanbase

We have now established that to grow rapidly with precision and scale, we need to search for medium-sized hills—a micro-vertical that can be won over one after another. Whether you're looking to break into a new industry or expand your customer base within a single industry, there is always more ground to cover and more hills to conquer!

So, how do you find a micro-vertical full of companies ready and willing to switch over to you?

If you're a new company, you'll likely choose the market with which you already have the most experience. After all, most founders create a business precisely because they are in an industry, see a problem, and develop a product or service to fix it. If this is you, your first step will start in the following chapter, where you'll learn how to turn your market insight into a decision-making tool.

However, if you're an established company with a list of existing customers, you'll want to start by probing deeper into that list. You just might find a sprouting fanbase you didn't realize existed. Let me give you an example.

Many times in my career, I have discovered clusters of highly similar customers right before me. The key is to be curious about data and patterns.

In Chapter One, I told you about working for Documentum, which sold sophisticated document management. As a reminder, the product was applicable to several markets. Still, we found success targeting the pharmaceutical industry, eventually becoming dominant in the New Drug Application (NDA) process.

In 1995, we were looking to gain more customers. One day,

after a visit to New York and a long conversation with a brilliant VP of sales, I looked again at our customer database. Besides the major group of pharmaceutical R&D clients we primarily served, I also noticed many banking customers—or, more specifically, companies labeled as "investment banks" or "universal banks" because they were so large that they did a bit of everything.

It was interesting, but these categories were extensive, and it didn't give me a vivid idea of what companies were in this category. I started organizing the data by different categories, getting increasingly more specific.

For New Companies Without a Target Market

If you're part of a new company with a horizontal product and no specific market in mind, I strongly urge against the "spray and pray" method: a marketing strategy that involves messaging to the masses, hoping it'll stick somewhere.

Instead, I urge you to evaluate potential micro-verticals described in the previous chapter: A *viable* micro-vertical for your team needs what you offer and is small enough to dominate but big enough to matter. Start by evaluating the micro-verticals your investors and ex-colleagues are part of, and conduct interviews with them using the methodology in the following chapter.

When, through the interviews, you find a micro-vertical that may be a good fit for you, take it as your test case. Run through the process this book will outline to determine if you want to pursue that hill or pivot elsewhere.

As I looked through the customer data, I noticed a pattern emerging. Each financial customer initially used Documentum to process transactions called "swaps and derivatives," which are huge-scale financial agreements between two parties without the supervision of a stock exchange. These transactions are called

Over-the-Counter (OTC) trades. A distinct segment within our banking customers was emerging.

What was strange and intriguing was that we had never spent a marketing dollar targeting these firms for this purpose, yet they all knew about us. We had a whole group of the most prestigious firms in the world using us to process multi-billion-dollar OTC trades. My wheels were turning now. We wanted to understand how this had happened.

After receiving the go-ahead, my team and I contacted several firms we considered thought leaders and set up a meeting.

In the meeting, we asked each firm, "How did you discover us, and how did you find our product a fit for your needs?"

Multiple expressed that they'd heard about us through word of mouth on Wall Street. That was incredible! Wall Street is not only one of the most prestigious places in the world, but it is a closely knit "village" of genius finance people who socialize and change jobs regularly.

We also learned that banks are universally implementing initiatives to reduce the risk associated with OTC contracts, which can become *incredibly* expensive for the bank if they take more than two days to process.

One executive remarked, "All these other software companies have been bragging that they can process OTC trades within two days. Then a colleague of mine said, 'Check out Documentum. They don't need two days. They can do it in minutes!' Well, that removed all the risk for us. It was a no-brainer."

We asked, "Where do you and your colleagues gather to share information and make recommendations like this?"

Each responded that the swaps and derivatives community has an association where everyone meets and socializes. It's called the ISDA (International Swaps and Derivatives Association).

I was fascinated. Seeing an opportunity, I asked, "Are there others in your association who might be willing to make the switch? And what might they be looking for?"

One responded, "You've already got what they're looking for. Plenty of other banks would switch over if they heard your pitch.

This group of people tends to move as a herd. Once one person finds a solution, word travels fast."

That was precisely what I wanted to hear: that we could increase our presence in this community without painful investment and see a massive return in tens of millions of dollars or more.

I left the interview feeling energized. When I considered expansion, I had imagined we might have to take on the industry giants—other financial services software firms—or invest lots of money in targeting a whole new community with which we didn't already have an inroad. We had already tried to tackle discrete manufacturing but failed. As it turned out, we already had a growing fan base on Wall Street right under our noses.

In the following months, I tailored a set of marketing plans specifically to the derivatives departments of the banks that led in these financial instruments but had not yet switched over. We made minor adjustments to process the rules associated with simple and complex derivatives best. Before long, almost every top-ranked derivatives bank in New York, London, and Frankfurt was using our product.

At Documentum, we found our group of medium-sized hills that we already had access to. A whole new micro-vertical market discovered us! After realizing this, all we had to do was notice and probe the pattern, and one customer after another fell into line.

Finding Micro-Verticals in Your Customer Database

What happened to me and Documentum was every marketing or sales executive's dream come true. We found some medium-sized hill companies we had already won over. Behind those hills was a whole collection of similar hills we could win with relatively little effort. What a gold mine!

Many companies do not realize that some medium-sized hills or ripe markets are already easily within reach. Even seasoned marketing executives can get caught up in the aforementioned battle plans—taking on all the new markets at once, taking on the big guns, or taking on a market they are not a good fit for—and miss these highly accessible markets right before them.

How does one find these ripe micro-verticals among your existing customers? We discover them by doing cluster analysis.

Cluster analysis is a method of processing customer data. You may or may not already be familiar with it. This method organizes the data into groups, which you then examine to see what insights might emerge from them.

You can use cluster analysis to analyze all types of data. But when analyzing groupings of companies and customers, a cluster represents a group of companies or customers closely associated with each other. In other words, when you see a cluster, you've found a micro-vertical! A set of hills that might have even more just behind them.

I have done this many times, and I did it with the customer data at Documentum. I organized the customers into groups based on industries, then created even more specific subgroups based on industry and/or how they used the product.

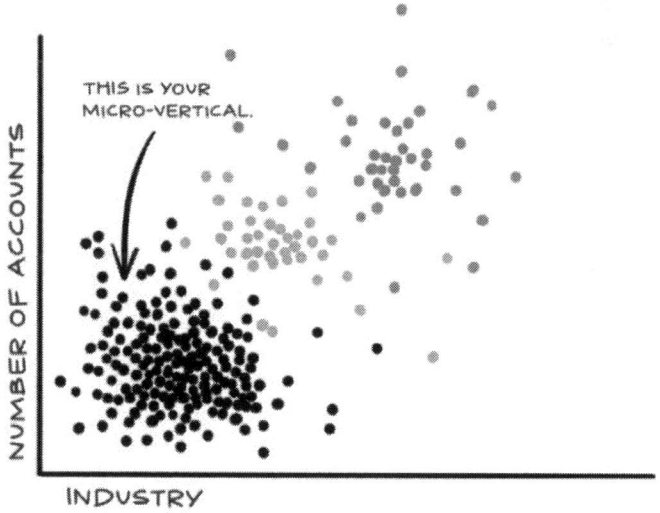

When I looked at the resulting clusters, some were as expected: big groups of bland categories such as "banking," but I also saw clusters I did not expect to see. These large, previously unnoticed clusters that were mostly untapped turned out to be the easiest ticket to big growth

Scoring vs. Qualifying Out Micro-Verticals

One common question I receive is how to choose one micro-vertical over another, especially if you find more than one viable cluster. Can we score potential micro-verticals?

Scoring does not help much in predicting success. What works better is to eliminate and *qualify out* micro-verticals based on their "red flags."

Once marketers start working on a micro-vertical, they tend to get attached and don't want to admit when it's not working out. Or they get excited about all the opportunities and don't want to miss out on any possibilities. But the best thing to do for yourself and your resources is to be choosy.

We will go deeper into what constitutes a red flag in the following chapters, and at the end of each, you'll be prompted with whether to pursue the micro-vertical, pause, or pivot (qualify out). We need not be afraid of qualifying out of a market. The whole point here is that plenty of other rich micro-verticals exist to explore. Permit yourself to walk away. When you do strike the perfect one, other hills will follow.

Cluster Analysis: Manual Versus GPT

If you're following me so far, you're likely now itching to know if you have an untapped micro-vertical hiding in plain sight. The good news is you don't need to wait for your new fan base of customers to find you. You can find them by performing a cluster analysis of your own.

Cluster analysis can be done manually, as I did in our earlier example. That said, it is laborious. If you're working with a large company, you may have thousands of customers to sort through. It's overwhelming to categorize by hand. Power users will typically export their customer data from their Customer Relationship Management (CRM) system into Excel, then try to manually group customers by industry. However, they will still encounter obstacles like the following:

- The industry categories are extensive (like "Finance" or "Insurance").
- The industry column has many blank spaces.
- There is no NAICS code for the companies you are looking for.
- Some companies fit into multiple categories, but only one is indicated.

This incomplete and ambiguous data makes it difficult to create precise groupings of similar companies with similar needs.

In these cases, users must manually fill in data for companies they recognize. With unrecognized companies, they need to go to every company or firm website, determine what kind of company it is, manually enter it into the spreadsheet, and create and consolidate their categories. After you've done all this, you have access to an extremely valuable data set where you can see untapped micro-verticals that were not evident before.

The process is differentiating, but it is also painful, not to mention expensive. In the pre-GPT era, I had data analytics teams of several people to clean up the data like this and make sense of it. Many companies—even large ones—do not have this kind of time or budget.

The ChatGPT Smart Conversation: Cluster Analysis

In the following section, I will walk you through a Smart Conversation with ChatGPT to find micro-verticals. When I first saw what ChatGPT-4o could do, I felt the scars from Darwinian analysis start to fade.

The results are truly incredible. But I didn't want to tell you how powerful this method is—I wanted to *show* you. I decided to showcase authentic Smart Conversations rooted in the real-life example of my current company, Sage.

Sage is a cloud-based financial management software company. I work with one of their products, which is called Intacct (the namesake of the company Sage acquired). We work with growing and mid-sized businesses, offering them the tools to modernize, streamline, and scale their financial systems.

In 2016, as the CMO of Intacct, I used a micro-vertical strategy to find new customers for us. I followed the method in this book, but without the use of Gen AI tools. I did the cluster analysis and all the following steps manually. We successfully found and won the new micro-vertical, but the plan took *three months* for my team to create.

I will conduct the following conversations as if I am in the same position, but this time, I am creating the plan in the present day using generative AI. The process no longer takes three months, that's for sure. Yet the quality is nearly the same if not better in some cases.

While I wrote this book in 2024 before I resumed working for Sage, I am thankful to them for allowing me to use my learnings from the company as our continuous example throughout the book's conversations.[2] Any private material will be fictionalized

---

[2] The fact that I now work for Sage, the company used in the examples, has in no way biased the conversation outcomes. During the research process, we confirmed ChatGPT to be a consistently objective responder (far more objective than a human analyst) regardless of what prompts we gave it or what companies we asked it to evaluate.

with synthetic data. However, the example will still allow you to see the power of the process and how it builds.

What we see here is very detailed, but the detail shows the incredible power of ChatGPT. A series of prompts alone does not do justice to what is happening. I did what previously took weeks to do in a few minutes—I got a decent, detailed segmentation that I could rely on. I assure you, you will not think about Excel the same way again!

This Is Not Real Data

I will include complete—or mostly complete—conversations with ChatGPT throughout this book. That is the best way for readers to witness its effectiveness firsthand, even if one doesn't have access to ChatGPT yet. In the real world, CRM data would be used for analysis. However, *this book contains no internal data from Sage or any real company.* Furthermore, the example throughout this book reflects our positioning from 2016, not from the present.

Unless otherwise stated, I have used synthetic data in all the cluster analyses and the book as a whole. Synthetic data is artificially generated data that mimics real-world data. It is created using algorithms and simulations that replicate the patterns and characteristics of genuine data without containing any actual sensitive information. This allows it to be used for testing, training machine learning models, and research purposes while protecting privacy concerns.

ChatGPT can create synthetic data if you'd like to experiment without using real data.

The conversation I had was as follows using ChatGPT-4o.

UPLOAD:
- A spreadsheet containing your customer names, websites, and respective industry labels (exported from your CRM). (For an extra layer of security, you can change the file name before you upload it to something anonymous like "Cluster Analysis test.")

PROMPT 0
Me: You are an industry marketing expert with specific experience in the segmentation of finance and insurance companies.

PROMPT 1
Me: How many industries are blank?

ChatGPT: There are 68 rows in the dataset where the "Industry" field is blank.

PROMPT 2
Me: Can you replace them with the correct industry where possible?

ChatGPT: To replace the blank "Industry" fields with the correct values, I'll need a mapping or a way to determine the correct industry for each entry. Do you have a list or a method to match the companies to their respective industries, or would you like me to attempt to infer the industry based on the company names and websites?

PROMPT 3
Me: Please infer where you can.

ChatGPT: I will attempt to infer the industries for the companies with missing values based on their names and websites. This process will involve some educated guesses based on common industry terms and website content. Let's proceed with this.

First, I'll identify the rows with missing industries and then infer the possible industries based on the account names and websites.

I have successfully inferred industries for all the rows where the "Industry" field was blank. Here is a summary:

- The number of rows with blank industries is now zero.
- The inferred industries are based on common keywords found in the account names and websites.

If you need any further adjustments or a detailed review of specific entries, please let me know!

I have generated a count of occurrences for each industry in the dataset. You can now review the industry distribution. If you need any additional analysis or adjustments, please let me know!

PROMPT 4

Me: "Finance & Insurance" and "Finance" are very broad categories. Can you analyze this category to be more specific?

ChatGPT: To refine the categories of "Finance & Insurance" and "Finance," I'll attempt to break these down into more specific subcategories based on the available data. This involves examining the account names and websites for additional context.

I'll create more granular subcategories within these broader categories, such as:
- Investment Banking

- Asset Management
- Financial Advisory
- Insurance Services
- Real Estate Finance
- Wealth Management

Let's proceed with this refinement.

It seems there is an issue with some of the "Account Name" or "Website" fields not being strings. I'll handle these cases and reapply the refinement process.

I have refined the categories within the "Finance & Insurance" and "Finance" industries. Here are the more specific subcategories and their counts:

- General Finance: 119
- Capital Management: 43
- Insurance Services: 10
- Investment Banking: 8
- Financial Advisory: 7
- Venture Capital: 6
- Trust Services: 5
- Asset Management: 3
- Wealth Management: 1
- Real Estate Finance: 1

Additionally, other categories and their counts remain unchanged.

If you need any further refinements or specific analyses, please let me know!

PROMPT 5
Me: Can you break this down to the next level of granularity?

ChatGPT: To break down the categories to the next level of granularity, I'll refine the subcategories further by identifying more specific types of services and industries within the already established categories. Here are some additional refinements I could consider:

- **General Finance**: Retail Banking, Corporate Banking, Financial Technology (FinTech)
- **Capital Management**: Private Equity, Hedge Funds, Asset Management
- **Insurance Services**: Life Insurance, Health Insurance, Property & Casualty Insurance
- **Investment Banking**: Mergers & Acquisitions, Underwriting, Sales & Trading
- **Financial Advisory**: Personal Financial Planning, Corporate Financial Planning, Tax Advisory
- **Venture Capital**: Early-Stage Venture, Late-Stage Venture, Seed Capital
- **Trust Services**: Estate Planning, Fiduciary Services, Custodial Services
- **Asset Management**: Mutual Funds, Portfolio Management, Wealth Management
- **Real Estate Finance**: Mortgage Services, Real Estate Investment Trusts (REITs)

Let's proceed with applying this next level of granularity to the dataset.

PROMPT 6

Me: Can you add a column that shows the next level of granularity and name the column "industry drilldown"?

ChatGPT: I have refined the categories further to the next level of granularity. Here are the counts for each specific subcategory:

- General Finance: 118
- Capital Management: 43

- Insurance Services: 10
- Consulting: 9
- Investment: 9
- Investment Banking: 8
- Financial Advisory: 7
- Venture Capital: 6
- Trust Services: 5
- Asset Management: 3
- Conglomerate: 3
- Management: 2
- Corporate Banking: 1
- Wealth Management: 1
- Real Estate Finance: 1
- Commodities: 1
- Engineering: 1
- Other: 15

If you need more detailed analysis or further refinements, please let me know!

PROMPT 7
Me: Can you add a column with NAICS codes?[3]

ChatGPT: I'll add a column with NAICS codes based on the refined industry categories. Here are some common NAICS codes that may be relevant:
- Retail Banking: 522110
- Corporate Banking: 522110
- Financial Technology: 541511
- Private Equity: 523910
- Hedge Funds: 523920
- Asset Management: 523920

---

[3] NAICS stands for North American Industry Classification System. This is a standardized system used to classify businesses by their type of economic activity for the sake of data collection and analysis.

- Life Insurance: 524113
- Health Insurance: 524114
- Property & Casualty Insurance: 524126
- Investment Banking: 523110
- Mergers & Acquisitions: 523110
- Underwriting: 523110
- Sales & Trading: 523120
- Personal Financial Planning: 523930
- Corporate Financial Planning: 523930
- Tax Advisory: 541213
- Early-Stage Venture: 523910
- Late-Stage Venture: 523910
- Seed Capital: 523910
- Estate Planning: 523920
- Fiduciary Services: 523991
- Custodial Services: 523991
- Mutual Funds: 523920
- Portfolio Management: 523920
- Wealth Management: 523920
- Mortgage Services: 522292
- Real Estate Investment Trusts (REITs): 531110

I'll now map these codes to the respective industries and add them to the dataset.

I have added a column with NAICS codes to the dataset based on the further refined industry categories. The data now includes the NAICS codes corresponding to each specific industry.

If you need any additional adjustments or further analysis, please let me know!

PROMPT 8
Me: Can you analyze NAICS codes, do a count by category, and display a graph?

ChatGPT:

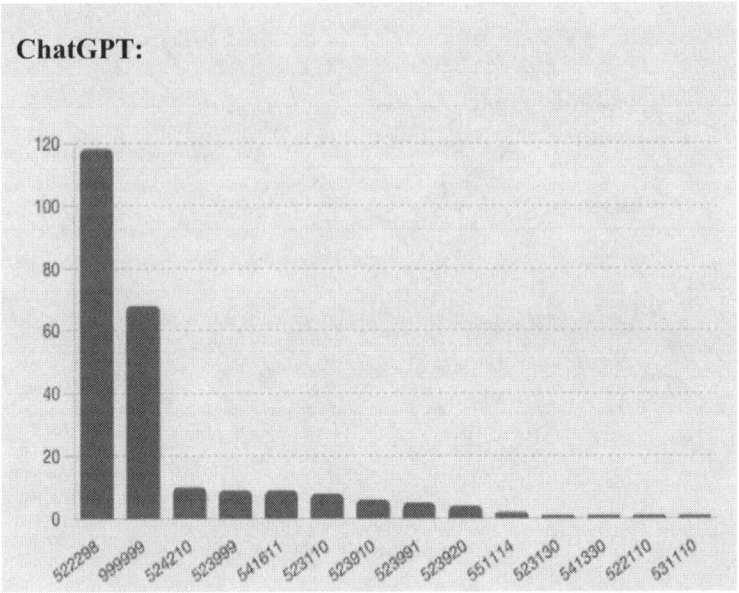

Here's what I'm thinking as I look at this chart. The first category is enormous because it is very general. But the second category is all unknown or unlabeled. There are about 63 companies labeled as #999999. There may be 50 small subcategories in this grouping—no significant cluster. Or this whole group may be one *colossal* cluster in itself. If it's all one category, how amazing would it be to realize that—and discover if there are even more!

I scanned the list of companies in this #999999 category, and I recognized some names. The ones I recognized are family offices.[4] I searched the Internet and easily found a list of the top 1,000 family offices. I uploaded it here so ChatGPT could cross-reference the lists and see how many unknown companies are family offices.

---

[4] A family office is a privately held company that manages the wealth and investments of a wealthy family—typically one that holds one hundred million to billions of dollars in investable assets. An office that caters to a single family is called a Single Family Office (SFO). An office that serves multiple wealthy families is called a Multi-Family Office (MFO).

PROMPT 9

Me: I have attached a publicly available list of family offices. Based on the website column, how many are in both spreadsheets?

ChatGPT: There are 49 websites that are common between the two datasets. This indicates that 49 family offices appear in both spreadsheets. If you need more detailed information or further analysis, please let me know!

Wow! Of the roughly 63 companies in the huge, unlabeled #999999 category, 49 are the same type of company! I have discovered a cluster that dwarfs all the others. While this is a synthetic data set, I have found clusters this big and bigger before.

A large cluster doesn't mean we've already covered the market. Rather, it indicates we are doing something very right in a market that is likely much, much bigger. There are probably hundreds, if not thousands, more to be won.

If the first type of company I checked had not turned out to be a significant cluster, I would have kept scanning the list for companies I recognized. When I recognized another category—say, Asset Management—I'd have found another top 1,000 list on the Internet for that industry, uploaded it to ChatGPT to cross-reference again, and repeated this process until I either found the most significant cluster or determined there is no large cluster here after all.

Even if this process takes multiple guesses, the process of guessing takes seconds or minutes. It is a minuscule investment of time that can generate enormous rewards

PROMPT 10
Me: Can you update the spreadsheet to say "family offices" for the 49 that appear?

ChatGPT: The spreadsheet has been updated to mark the 49 common entries as "family offices" in the "Industry" column. You can download the updated file from the link below:

If you need any further modifications or analysis, please let me know!

PROMPT 11
Me: Can you do a count by industry?

ChatGPT: I have provided the updated count of occurrences for each industry in the dataset. You can now review the updated industry distribution.

If you need further analysis or additional modifications, please let me know!

Conversation Highlights

Bingo: cluster discovered!

Of course, one must continue to think for themselves and analyze what ChatGPT produces during the conversation. But as a conversational partner, this tool is pretty fantastic.

This response perfectly aligns with what I discovered while doing manual cluster analysis for Intacct several years ago. I also found that family offices were a significant cluster in which we could invest more heavily. We eventually won this micro-vertical. The difference? Manually discovering this cluster took weeks, while this conversation revealed the same discovery in a matter of minutes.

The response to Prompt 9 especially blew my mind. Prompt 9 was when I asked ChatGPT to compare a publicly available list of family offices to my customer list. Before this, each family office on my list had an incorrect or nonexistent category for "Industry."

Manually discovering this cluster took weeks, while this conversation revealed the same discovery in a matter of minutes.

However, ChatGPT could cross-reference its working dataset with another spreadsheet and use its findings from the web to identify the overlaps between the two. For the database nerds here, joining two spreadsheets without ever going into Excel and doing a "VLOOKUP" is astounding!

What this means is you can now do cluster analysis on *any* list, including those that do not have an industry category. If you didn't find the cluster on your first try, you could ask it to cross-reference other industries to find the cluster. For example, you could say:

- "I have attached a publicly available list of Fortune 500 companies. Based on the website, how many are in both spreadsheets?"
- "I have attached a publicly available list of early-stage, industry-focused Private Equity firms. Based on the website, how many are in both spreadsheets?"

This series of prompts took a few minutes to execute compared to weeks of analysis going to website after website. Now, anytime you see a large cluster of "Unknowns" in your data set, they will be easy to classify. And they may identify a micro-vertical with excellent growth potential!

45

Key Output from Step 1

After performing cluster analysis, you should have:

- A list of both major and minor clusters (micro-verticals) within your existing customer base—with a complete audit trail of how you got them
- For each cluster, an industry identification and ranking
- Identification of the biggest and potentially most valuable clusters

CHAPTER 4
Your AI Customer Advisory Board

If you're currently working for an established business and you have just finished the previous chapter, you may be entering this chapter having just discovered a micro-vertical—a well of untapped opportunity from your very own customer base. Or perhaps you have already decided through other means on a market you want to take over. This chapter will take you through the next step toward winning that market.

If you are a new company looking to establish yourself in the micro-vertical you likely had in mind when you created the company, this is your first step. This step will set you up for new market domination on par with the big players. It will utilize any previous experience, insight, and connections you have in the industry already—especially including any hands-on experience you have with the major needs your customers are facing. This chapter is your perfect starting point for turning these insights into a strategy.

No matter the scale of your company, winning over a micro-vertical starts with one irreplaceable step: understanding the customer. That is not breaking news to those in marketing, but that doesn't mean marketers always heed this truth. Companies often run broad, sweeping campaigns on a very shallow understanding of any individual group within their reach. Instead of reaching a vast audience with minimal investment, like these campaigns purport, they only prove to each audience that the company does not "get them" at all.

The level of customer understanding needs to be even deeper when targeting a micro-vertical. When targeting a cluster like this, you are speaking to a very niche group (that may well be a large group) of industry insiders. They have unique communal language, pains, joys, goals, and information networks. They can call you out within seconds if you don't speak their language.

I could compare this to being a soccer fan in America. I've been living here for decades, so American football has had its chance to woo me, but I'll never get more excited than when I am watching the Champions League—a league of the best teams in Europe. Soccer fans know the major teams, which ones are at the top at that moment, who the top scorers are, and we understand the meaning of terms like "hat trick" or "offside." We know what on earth the Ballon d'Or is. When the World Cup comes around, I can tell within seconds whether the person I'm discussing it with is part of my community or just following the headlines.

A true fan also knows the pain of being a soccer fan living in America. It's one thing when one's team is doing poorly. But one of the most frustrating pains is not even being able to watch your team play live! Insiders know you can only catch most games on Paramount+ and have to subscribe in a particular way to access the proper channels. To show you what it's like being a soccer fan here requires a very niche understanding of all these things.

The same is true for customers in these niche, micro-vertical industries. To show that you *get them* and their work, you need to speak their industry's language, learn their terms, know their big names, favorite resources, and networks, and understand what they need.

How do you get this kind of insider understanding? The tried and true way of gaining insight into them is through customer interviews. And even though I will give you an expedited way to go about this stage using ChatGPT, I still can't overstate the value of starting with detailed customer interviews.

I have done a lot of interviewing in my life, and I can think of countless times when a customer interview provided invaluable decision-making insights. One such time was when I served as CMO of Argyle Data. Argyle Data was a company trying to find new ways of detecting telecommunication fraud. At the time, it was a tiny startup trying to determine how its product fit into the equation.

Our team was working to discover fraud in real time through AI. We were the AI experts, and the leading company funding us, our first customers, were the fraud experts. We wanted to understand the fraud problem better to see if our AI mechanisms could stop it more quickly. After all, we knew the telecommunications industry already had fraud prevention. We needed to understand what our AI system could do that the legacy system could not.

One day, I got to talk on the phone with the Head of Fraud at the country level.

I had been researching ahead of time and learning about one of the most common fraud techniques: A bad actor would call a number, hang up after one ring, then wait until the other person called them back. When the other person called them back, that person was now on a call costing them ten dollars per *minute* because of the type of phone number the perpetrators had set up. At that time, the cost of these calls was around two billion dollars globally, and the telecom company's users were paying for them.

I asked the Head of Fraud, "I've been reading about this fraud technique. Can you tell me more about it? How does it bypass the anti-fraud barriers already in place?"

She proudly responded, "Yes, well, we have many effective anti-fraud protections in place." But I could hear the exasperation creep into her voice as she sighed and went on. "We have these rules-based systems based on our fraud research. For example, if a number does five ring-and-hang-up calls in under ten minutes, we block it. But the criminals will prod our system. They will fail against it until they figure it out and find its limits. Then, they'll come in just under the radar. They'll do four calls in under ten minutes instead of five. They're barely under the threshold for our 'fraud radars,' so they succeed—every time."

Her response immediately gave me a deeper insight into their rules system. I was aware of a rules system and that it's easy to keep adding rules, so beforehand, I didn't quite understand why their prevention methods weren't working. Our conversation confirmed that the rules system was a losing battle in which they could only ever stay a single step ahead, at best, with the criminals always right on their heels, figuring out rule by rule.

For Argyle, this conversation confirmed that AI fraud prevention was the way forward. I went on to interview several more telecom companies. I learned more about their pain points and how we could tailor our product to address their challenges more effectively.

With this insight from interviews, we developed the best technology in the world to do what it did. We became the telecom fraud partner of choice of Cloudera, the biggest "Big Data" company in the world at the time. The company was quickly acquired by Mavenir. But in those early days, the interview process was what crystallized the role we could play in solving billion-dollar pain points.

Creating Your Ideal Customer Profile

We used a particular tool to turn fifty customer interviews into a condensed, actionable guide for decision-making: an Ideal Customer Profile (ICP). If you're in the marketing world, you've likely heard this term.

An **Ideal Customer Profile (ICP)** describes the customer who would most benefit from your product or service. In turn, these are also the most lucrative customers for your business. The ICP is a fictional character or business, but it represents and consolidates the most essential elements from your real customers. To make this more concrete, look at your list of companies in the cluster you found in the last chapter or companies you know of in the market you want to win.

Each industry and company has its language, needs, etc., and each has a buyer. A common mistake, even among professionals, is assuming the buyer is one company or person. Nowadays, the buyer is most often a buying *team*. The buying team is responsible for researching, evaluating, and purchasing products or services the company needs. The buying team could be two or three people at a smaller company. In a larger enterprise, the buying team often comprises six to eight people, including members from different departments like finance, operations, IT, and management. Each buying team member also has their unique terms, pain points, goals, and priorities.

The buying team members form what I call an **ICP Chain of Pain**: The pains of the members at the top trickle down through the whole organization, layer by layer. If the CEO is hurting, that pain trickles to the next person, perhaps the CFO, with a sentiment like, "I don't care how you do it; just do it!" That pain seeps down to the accountant or controller who receives a similar message. Pain flows downward. Soon enough, the whole organization fixes the pain throughout the chain.

To dominate a market, you need to understand the pain points of the industry and company—as well as the pains of *each* buying team member. The CEO needs to hear that you can fix their most prominent issues. The CFO must know if the financial systems can support the CEO's strategy. Then the accountant or controller wants to see if they can switch to your system without pulling an all-nighter to transfer all the data by hand.

> To dominate a market, you need to understand the pain points of the industry and company—as well as the pains of *each* buying team member.

The driver behind this stage is to gain as deep an understanding as possible about the company—or companies—you want to target in your micro-vertical of choice. So, in addition to details on the company, the ICP also includes buyer personas for each member of the buying team. We want to know who has power, what they are like, what they need, how we can access them, and *what will win them over*.

The ICP includes a range of detailed information:
- Firmographics: company size, annual revenue, number of employees
- A set of buyer personas

The personas include:
- Demographics: buyers' age, gender, education, income, industry, company size, and job role
- Geographic information: where buyers live and operate their business
- Psychographics: buyers' needs, pain points, goals, attitudes
- Behaviors: how the buyers use technology, how fast they make changes

Creating an ICP, complete with details on each ideal buyer, is extremely valuable for companies of any size. Of course, it does not provide an exhaustive list of potential customer attributes—but that is the point. Its specific and focused nature provides a clear target for businesses to aim for. It helps marketing and sales teams ensure their efforts are always made with the most important and lucrative customers in mind.

Creating Your ICP: Manual Versus ChatGPT

How do you create your ICP? Historically, as I did with Sage, an ICP is developed by conducting many interviews and identifying patterns. The patterns then form the template, which is the ICP.

Simple. Well, sort of. The process is simple. The *practice* is incredibly laborious and time-intensive. As you may recall, I interviewed *fifty* family office customers. Do you know how long it takes to track down and set up meetings with *fifty* different busy professionals? It can take days of texting and rescheduling to meet a friend for brunch. Then I met with each of the fifty for a full hour. For each interview, I took five to seven pages of typed notes. I compared those notes with association research, analyst reports, and blogs, contacted the customer for any follow-up questions, and condensed each interview's notes to two pages.

Once I completed the interviews, I had *one hundred* pages of notes to scan for patterns manually. I reserved a conference room in Sage's building and dragged desks from the surrounding rooms. I lined them up end-to-end until I had a work surface spanning over fifteen feet. I laid the hundred-plus pages out on the tables and went down the line highlighting specific patterns in different colors. Yellow for time. Pink for cost. Green for risk. That took me around twenty-four hours spread across a couple of days before I eventually came out of my cave with a clear set of patterns and insights that comprised our new family office ICP.

This process was incredibly valuable, and the results spoke for themselves. But I do not envy my past self and the late nights I spent dozing off on spreadsheets in that conference room—nor would I ever do it this way today. It is simply no longer necessary with the resources now available. This approach is not feasible for most companies' time and budget. And even if it's successful, this approach is challenging to scale and repeat for multiple micro-verticals.

For the AI beginner, conducting all the interviews and then plugging the notes or transcripts into ChatGPT to analyze and identify the patterns might make the manual process easier. This alone would save hours—maybe even days or weeks! And this alone would be akin to a miracle in the desert for my past self sifting through all those interviews.

However, a ChatGPT native would realize this is a severe underutilization of the tool. I came to this realization while writing this book. I began to wonder: Could I get the same quality of customer insights without the laborious process of conducting fifty interviews? The answer is yes.

One day, I wondered how much customer info ChatGPT could get me based on the public LinkedIn profile of someone I would typically interview. I chose a company and pulled up the LinkedIn profiles of a handful of their executives who would likely be on the buying team: the CEO, CRO, CMO, CIO (Chief Investment

Officer), and CISO (Chief Information & Security Officer). I downloaded their public profiles as PDFs and fed them into ChatGPT; then, I began asking questions I would typically ask the interviewee.

The results floored me. I have been conducting these interviews for decades, and the insights I got from this Smart Conversation with ChatGPT gave me at least 80% of the insights I typically would have gotten from a one-hour conversation.

I still think person-to-person interviews are incredibly valuable; they provide insight and connection that one cannot get from an AI exchange. However, I now do around five interviews rather than fifty. I then use ChatGPT to help me match the power of fifty interviews while using hardly a fraction of the time it used to take.

For you, I recommend an approach that combines the strengths of manual interviews with the incredible power of ChatGPT. Even a few manual interviews with top customers can check or validate ChatGPT's findings, making your ICP more precise. Of course, they also help you become interpersonally connected to key market members you want to access.

That said, if you have no customers willing to be interviewed, or you do not have the resources to invest in interviews, you can rely on ChatGPT alone—with LinkedIn profiles and case studies—to get roughly 80% of the same insight. That's still quite impressive and useful to get you started.

Manual Interview Masterclass

Since I recommend integrating three to five real customer interviews into this process—and I have observed far too many time-wasting interviews in my day—I will dedicate a brief section here on how to get the most out of customer interviews.[5] Then, we'll

---

[5] If you did not start out with cluster analysis but chose a market through other means, I recommend you do 5–10 interviews to be extra sure your understanding is accurate and well-rounded.

move into the Smart Conversation, showing how to multiply the interviews' impact tenfold.

When I worked as the CMO for the software company Alfresco in 2007, I got deep into podcasting and conducted many interviews with customers and experts. Through this experience, I learned a deep value for interviewing and developed a tailored customer interview methodology. The following is not a sales or case study script but a market discovery script. It tries to tease out the good, the bad, and the ugly.

The methodology is designed to identify the customer's qualities and needs and make it clear if this market is not a good fit for you. It's better to discover the issues now rather than after the product has been launched and have customers on the phone demanding their money back.

Overarching Principles:

- Aim for three to five in-depth interviews—roughly sixty minutes each.
- Use the same interview process and structure for all customer interviews.
- Never ask a question that can be answered with a yes or a no.
- When talking with the customer, avoid marketing speak (e.g., "early adopter," "visionary," "compelling reason to buy," etc.).
- Make the interview feel as much like a conversation over a glass of wine as an interview.
- Schedule interviews as close to one another as possible to get a feel for patterns. It is hard to discern when interviews are weeks apart.
- Do not outsource or delegate the interview process to a junior person. An interview is an opportunity to get to know your most strategic asset: your best customers.
- After the customer interview, note whether the interviewee had a fascinating story, was particularly articulate, or both. The ones that match both are your future spokespeople.

The Preparation Process
- Research the person, company, or firm ahead of time; look at their LinkedIn profile, posts, blog, articles, annual reports, etc.
- Get a basic understanding of their landscape, the market shift they are facing, and—if they are a customer—how they're using your product/services.

The Interview
- Frame the conversation.
  - "[Name] recommended I speak with you. They said you were using our product in an interesting way. We are interviewing our most innovative customers to help us drive strategy and product direction."
- Put the customer at ease with a simple question.
  - "Can you describe your company/firm and tell me any interesting nuances about it?"
- Clarify how they use your product/service.
  - "Can you describe what you were using before? Do you use any other products or extensions alongside ours?"
- Discover the "why switch, why now, why us."
  - "People put up with these pain points for years. What was your final straw?" (You are searching to see if the impetus for the switch is particular to the customer or is common to the whole industry; the latter is a goldmine.)
- Discover market awareness and perception.
  - "How did you hear about us? What resources do you read to keep up with industry trends? What associations do you belong to? What is your industry's perception of us? How would you describe us to a colleague?"
- Ask questions that identify your value.
  - "Did our product/service save you time? Reduce cost? Reduce risk? Increase growth?"

- Discover metrics.
  - "What are the key industry metrics you use?"
- Discover whole product requirements.
  - "What other products do you think are critical to integrate into our products/services in a perfect world?"
- Discover the real competition.
  - "What other products have you used or looked at? How would you compare the various systems, and why did you choose us (if they did)"?
- Determine if there is motivation to switch.
  - "When you examine your key challenges and needs, which ones are compelling to do now versus next year? What is the impact of not doing them?"
- End with open questions.
  - "Can you describe your perfect world? If there is one thing we could do to be more successful in your space, what would it be? Is there any question I have not asked that you think I should have?"

If this interview process is done well and the same general questions are asked in each interview, the rest is relatively straightforward. You don't even need to scan for the patterns manually. You can upload them to inform and validate the creation of your ICP with ChatGPT.

The ChatGPT Smart Conversation: Developing the Ideal Customer Profile

The following Smart Conversation is a continuation of the previous chapter's conversation. As a reminder, here is what we know from the conversation so far:

- I am chatting as a marketing leader searching for growth opportunities for Sage's product, Sage Intacct.

- ChatGPT helped me identify that family offices were a massive cluster among our existing customers that I could target further with minimal effort and high reward.

Now, ChatGPT will help me create an ICP to understand the remaining family offices I want to target.

Typically, you would create your ICP using the advice of dozens of your ideal customers. In the following Smart Conversation, ChatGPT functions as those customers, using the public information available and any other information you have given it. ChatGPT effectively becomes your Customer Advisory Board, accessible 24/7 for all your questions.

Whether you did full interviews or have nothing but company names, ChatGPT can enrich data enormously to increase the precision of its responses. Whatever additional documents you can upload to ChatGPT will help it enrich your data. Here's what I recommend: Choose a few companies in your cluster, type their names into a search engine, and gather the names of big players at that company. Look for people with a C before their title: CEO, CRO, CMO, CIO, CISO, etc. Find their public LinkedIn profiles and download them (seven to ten or more) in PDF format. You will feed these into ChatGPT before entering Prompt 1.[6]

In addition to LinkedIn profiles, you can also upload public bios, customer posts, interview articles, case studies on company websites, and public presentations. Comparison sites can generate PDFs of competitive assessments. Company reports can be uploaded as well.

In this way, a GPT can be used as a workspace in which you collect key documents to create your ICP. A GPT can store up to twenty files at once. These can also be uploaded before Prompt 1, or you can continue uploading new material and having ChatGPT update the ICP based on what you've added.

---

[6] If you already have customers in the micro-vertical you want to target, include the LinkedIn profiles of the existing customers whom you want more customers like. If you don't have customers already, you can use the profiles of people who would be your ideal customers.

With Smart Conversations like this, individual, team, and company personas can be built quickly and easily. The conversation can begin.

UPLOAD:

- PDF LinkedIn Profiles of seven to ten decision makers in the market you want to target
- Optional: transcripts of any manual interviews you may have done
- Optional: any public case studies about the micro-vertical
- Optional: any public bios, details from comparison sites, customer posts, interview articles, public presentations, or company reports that might give further insight into the ideal customer

PROMPT 0
Me: You are an expert at developing industry marketing plans for the family offices market after having worked in that space for twenty years.

PROMPT 1
Me: I need to create an Ideal Customer Profile for the buying team based on the attached customer profiles. Browse the web for any family office public case studies, press articles on family office customers, blogs on family office customers, or other family office customer reference materials from third parties. Do you have enough information to complete the task?

ChatGPT: Based on the documents provided and additional research, here's an Ideal Customer Profile (ICP) for family offices considering investment management solutions:

Ideal Customer Profile (ICP): Family Offices in Invest-ment Management

- **Organization Type:**
  - Single-family offices (SFOs): Managing the wealth and investments of one affluent family.
  - Multi-family offices (MFOs): Serving multiple high-net-worth families with diverse investment needs.
- **Assets Under Management (AUM):**
  - Typically ranging from $500 million to several billion dollars.
- **Investment Focus:**
  - Private Equity: Direct investments in private companies.
  - Real Estate: Commercial, residential, and mixed-use properties.
  - Alternative Investments: Hedge funds, venture capital, and other non-traditional assets.
- **Geographic Presence:**
  - Operations primarily in North America, with potential investments globally.
- **Organizational Structure:**
  - Multiple legal entities or LLCs for different investment vehicles.
  - Complex ownership structures requiring detailed consolidation and reporting.
- **Key Challenges:**
  - Consolidation: Efficiently consolidating financials across multiple entities.
  - Reporting: Generating timely and accurate reports for stakeholders.
  - Compliance: Adhering to regulatory requirements across jurisdictions.
  - Data Management: Integrating data from various sources for comprehensive analysis.

- **Decision-Making Team:**
  - Chief Financial Officer (CFO): Oversees financial strategy and operations.
  - Chief Investment Officer (CIO): Manages investment portfolios and strategies.
  - VP of Operations: Ensures operational efficiency and process optimization.
  - Family Members: Principals or beneficiaries involved in decision-making.
- **Technology Needs:**
  - Integrated Accounting Systems: To manage multi-entity consolidations and shared charts of accounts.
  - Dashboard and Reporting Tools: For real-time financial insights and performance tracking.
  - Data Integration Capabilities: To streamline information from various investment platforms.
- **Service Requirements:**
  - Customization: Solutions tailored to unique family office structures and investment strategies.
  - Scalability: Systems that accommodate growth and diversification of investments.
  - Support and Training: Ongoing assistance to ensure effective utilization of technology.
- **Goals and Objectives:**
  - Wealth Preservation: Maintaining and growing family wealth across generations.
  - Operational Efficiency: Reducing manual processes and improving accuracy.
  - Strategic Growth: Identifying and capitalizing on new investment opportunities.

This ICP reflects the typical characteristics and needs of family offices in the investment management sector, guiding targeted marketing and solution development efforts.

PROMPT 2
Me: Can you expand on the buying team? Specifically, their role, influence in the buying process, major pains, significant requirements, and backgrounds?

ChatGPT:
- **Family Principal – Patriarch**
  o Role: Ultimate decision maker, Delegate recommendation to CFO
  o Major Pains: Wealth transfer and preservation
  o Major Requirements: Simple insights and dashboards with multi-asset reporting. White glove services
  o Background: Self-made entrepreneur, investor, or heir
- **Chief Investment Officer (CIO)**
  o Role: Key decision maker for investment-related products
  o Major Pains: Portfolio complexity—real estate, private equity, public equities, venture capital & potentially hedge funds
  o Major Requirements: Consolidated multi-asset reporting
  o Background: Ex-investment. Banker, private equity, or hedge fund
- **Chief Financial Officer (CFO)**
  o Role: Key decision maker on financial solutions
  o Major Pains: Manual accounting & reconciliation, family offices often rely on spreadsheets and outdated software
  o Major Requirements: Multi-entity consolidation across real estate, private equity, public equities, venture capital, and potentially hedge funds. Protection of financial data from natural disaster

- o Background: CPA, CFA, MBA with experience in corporate finance, accounting, or auditing. Often, ex-Big Four accounting firm
- **Accountant**
  - o Role: Close the books
  - o Major Pains: Reliance on spreadsheets or outdated products
  - o Major Requirements: Modern cloud accounting software removing the need for consolidation in a spreadsheet
  - o Background: CPA, CFA, MBA from a top school
- **Next-Generation Family Members**
  - o Role: Young, pushing for digital transformation, AI, and automation
  - o Major Pains: Resistance to new technology by older family members
  - o Major Requirements. User-friendly digital platform making wealth management accessible
  - o Background: Tech-savvy

Overall Key Challenges:

- Consolidation – Efficiently consolidating financials across multiple entities, including situations where there is partial ownership
- Reporting – Generating timely and accurate reports for stakeholders
- Compliance – Adhering to regular requirements across jurisdictions
- Data Integration – Integrating data from various sources for comprehensive analysis

Conversation Highlights

This conversation was much shorter, though it can easily be elongated with follow-up questions. That said, this response was incredible given the limited input and time spent on this part of the process. ChatGPT was able to extract this behavioral and psychographic data, all from what is publicly available, in minutes.

ChatGPT identified the entire buying team and Chain of Pain in the above responses. We can see a theme stemming from the top of the chain: The head of the family, or the Family Principal, wants to see multi-asset reporting. In other words, they want to see a more diverse portfolio of assets—but one that they can still observe and track with the same amount of ease. But we also see the pain trickle down as the rest of the buying team works to meet that demand: The CIO struggles to create compliant reports of all these assets; the CFO struggles with the financial accounting for the new influx of assets; the accountant struggles to close the books using a simple Excel sheet—all while the next-gen family members demand a more modern and transparent digital platform.

All this is spot-on. When I manually researched the family office sector several years ago, I did roughly *fifty* interviews to get this level of understanding of the ICP and the Chain of Pain. With Smart Conversations, I only need to do a few, if any! Just imagine the time this saves. Now, knowing intimately about our ICP and each team member's pain, we know what would motivate each of them to buy now. Even better, you can continually load in more customer profiles, customer interviews, or stories and continue to ask questions and get insightful responses. The power comes from combining the mass of scraped data with minimal publicly available personal information.

Key Output from Step 2

After this conversation about your ideal customer, you should have:

- An ICP representing companies in the micro-vertical you want to target
- A customer persona for each member of the ICP's buying team
- An understanding of the ICP Chain of Pain (what will motivate *each member* to buy?)
- A rational idea of whether you should
  - Pursue: Your product/service fits the ICP's needs in this micro-vertical.
  - Pause: Do further research to see if this micro-vertical is a fit for you.
  - Pivot: Your product/service does not fit the ICP's needs; you have qualified out this micro-vertical and can now explore others.

CHAPTER 5
Spotting Seismic Market Shifts

In the previous step, you gained a deeper understanding of your micro-vertical of interest. Based on your Smart Conversation and any interviews you conducted, you now have an ICP and a set of personas for the key decision makers on the buying team. If, from this understanding, you've determined you are a good fit for this group's needs, you're ready to move on to the next step.

The next step is to consider this: I know why my ideal customer would switch to my product or service. *But do they have any motivation to switch now?*

Identifying your ideal customer's pain points is critical, but as we all know, having pain doesn't necessarily mean you're ready to take action that would alleviate it. Acting often involves making a change—sometimes a major infrastructural or systemic change. Change is a pain in itself—a pain that sometimes trumps all others and keeps the ICP from switching even if what you're offering them is objectively better.

Much of my professional experience is in cloud-based software, so let me give you an example from that realm. Before 2020, cloud-based software was widespread but not nearly as ubiquitous as now. Countless companies still opted for local data storage. You'd install the necessary software onto a Mac or PC and typically keep it in the office.

Cloud storage was (and is) better for various reasons: If your data were kept in the cloud, you wouldn't lose it in a disaster like a fire or a hurricane. You wouldn't have to install updates; it would upgrade automatically. It would also make data shareable regardless of one's physical location.

All that said, local storage still got the job done. Sure, it was an aging system. However, changing one's entire accounting system would be like subjecting the company to open heart surgery. Even if it's needed, it's a vast and disruptive undertaking. So, these many aches and pains were put off and put off longer by many executives who weren't willing to pause production and put their company on the operating table.

However, a seismic shift happened in 2020: the pandemic. Suddenly, people couldn't go to the office. Even if they took their machines home, they couldn't share information with each other in the ways they needed. Businesses relying on local storage screeched to a halt.

I would say, "My phone was ringing off the hook," but there was no hook because I, too, was working from home, trying not to bother my wife with the unending string of Zoom calls. In some ways, I felt like an ER doctor who suddenly had a very long line. Each company desperately needed an emergency surgery to switch to the cloud, or the business was going to die.

Discovering a Discontinuity

An event like the pandemic is one pronounced example of a phenomenon called a **discontinuity**. A discontinuity (also known as a **market shift**) is when, due to a sudden change, a whole industry has to immediately embrace a new way of doing things. It shifts the entire landscape—the companies must *discontinue* business as usual, or they may quickly cease to exist. Sometimes, as in the case of COVID-19, the shift is large enough to shake several industries at once. The pandemic presented businesses across countless industries with a discontinuity that forced them to switch to cloud-based software if they wanted to survive.

While an international crisis certainly counts as a cross-industry discontinuity, discontinuities can be caused by other forces as well. The invention of the iPhone is an example of a discontinuity caused by a technology shift.[7] This innovation also affected multiple industries: any company relying on customers finding them through the Internet. After this shift, people were not always using computers to view company websites; they were using mobile browsers and apps. Websites and programs built for computer screens looked terrible on an iPhone. So if companies wanted to continue attracting customers, they needed to pivot toward a mobile-friendly and/or app-based approach or risk going out of business. They needed to hire an app developer or someone who could program a website for mobile use. App developers hugely benefited from this discontinuity, as did early adopters of mobile-first design.

Discontinuities can also be driven by regulatory shifts unique to the micro-vertical. The rollout of HIPAA is one example.[8] Starting in 2003 and developing until 2013, HIPAA regulations were intended to ensure medical conversations were encrypted and to restrict and audit who looks at what. Driven by sweeping forces outside their control, hospitals, primary care physicians, and everybody connected in the medical field suddenly needed to implement robust technological safeguards, create systems to assess risk, train staff, and potentially hire someone internally to oversee their HIPAA compliance. They were forced to overhaul their systems or risk being shut down. This presented a massive boom in business for consultants, software, auditors, and security companies to build and facilitate these new systems.[9]

Discontinuities are enormous opportunities, but they may seem too rare to strategize around. After all, it's not every day that someone invents the next iPhone or a pandemic sweeps the nation.

---

[7] Other examples of technology shifts include the advent of the internet, AI, generative AI, relational databases, and war drones, to name just a few.

[8] HIPPA, the Healthcare Insurance Portability and Accountability Act, is a federal law that implemented nationwide standards on protecting individuals' sensitive health and medical information.

[9] Other examples of industry-specific shifts include Covid in the restaurant business, the shift toward real estate investments in family offices, BASEL II regulations in financial services, and the shift to generic drug prescriptions.

But while it's true they don't happen every day, they are much more common than one might think. The vast majority of discontinuities are simply ones the public never hears about because they only affect a niche industry—or even a subset of that industry. And while they're not flashy enough to make the news, these shifts are still enormous and pressing for a substantial group of customers. They are happening constantly if you know how to look for them, as we'll discuss here.

When you are looking to expand your business, discovering a micro-vertical is great, but discovering a micro-vertical going through a discontinuity is even better. Understanding the market shift is the key to winning the hearts and minds of not just one customer at a time but a whole group of customers with the same needs.

That said, many marketing and sales professionals struggle to identify a true discontinuity. Marketers will get over-excited to hear about a potential customer's pains and think, "They surely can't go on like this. This has got to be a discontinuity. We've got this customer in the bag." Yet they forget that people have short-term memory loss. When the customers have closed the books in accounting, done their business planning, etc., they will *swear* they'll never go through that again. A month later, they have forgotten about the pain, and it continues as an annual ritual. The pain of switching becomes more real and stressful than the existing system. This is not a discontinuity; this is a misguided "happy ears" moment: getting over-excited because you only heard what you wanted to hear.

Marketers can also get misguided "happy ears" over a significant shift halting business as usual—but only for one company. This often occurs when a CFO gets fired or there is some other staff change. Or there is a major mistake made in the current system that can never happen again. When the shift affects only one company, it is called a **trigger event**. As in, the event triggers a widespread change in the business. This is good to notice but still only yields one new customer at a time. It is *not* a discontinuity.

Here is the criterion for a true discontinuity:

- It impacts not just one company but an entire group of companies within a cluster.
- It impacts enough of their daily operations that it brings business as usual to a halt.
- If the company does not find a new system, it risks going out of business or becoming irrelevant.
- The companies must act now (not next year).

In nearly all cases, when a micro-vertical experiences a market shift, its members want to move in the same way as others in their cluster. These companies are already in a vulnerable, transitional moment. They want to minimize further risk and get into their new normal as quickly as possible. If someone has already found a solution and implemented it successfully, the first customers will spread the word among their networks. The following companies will come in droves.

WHEN THE MARKET SHIFTS,
CUSTOMERS MUST LEAP—
OR RISK THE FALL.

Optimizing on a Discontinuity

While a discontinuity represents a crisis for some, it represents an opportunity for others. If you have the solution to a whole industry's "hair on fire" problem, you are doing them a great service by clearly and swiftly presenting that solution to them. And of course, you stand to gain a whole new cluster of customers—perhaps multiple clusters, as the adjacent industries (or hills) likely have similar needs. This pursuit is mutually beneficial.

I have reviewed many marketing plans, and this is one of the biggest mistakes I find: The team has identified a true discontinuity, but for whatever reason, they do not even mention it in the messaging. They have the remedy to the crisis but put forth an entirely different positioning statement.

Often, this huge miss is because teams are going to market with a horizontal approach; they don't want to be too specific because they want to present themselves to as many affected companies as possible. They want to increase their TAM. Yet in broadening the approach, these marketers dilute their relevancy until it's nonexistent. Customers tune them out. You are selling aspirin for everyone, but the buyer has their hair on fire. They don't want your aspirin when others speak their language and offer a hose to put out the fire.

If you truly want to optimize around the potential of the discontinuity, your messaging and positioning to the potential customer need to revolve around their discontinuity. If the discontinuity is that their data center burned down in a wildfire, don't sit there and flaunt your latest features. Tell them that if they switch to the cloud, this type of loss will never happen to them again. Tell them you will eliminate their risk of losing data to another natural disaster. If the regulatory shift is new ESG (Environment, Social, Governance) standards, consultancies should be direct: Tell businesses you will fix their ESG problem—you will measure their environmental/social impact and help them become compliant.

This is what my team and I did during the pandemic. I was working for Sage as their head of marketing for Intacct. Once peo ple found out they couldn't go into the office, the "hair on fire" need was to switch to cloud software and get their businesses up and running remotely. Knowing this, we didn't focus our marketing messages on flaunting our new features. We focused our messaging on the problem: "You need to get on the cloud. We'll take you there." Speaking to the market shift and presenting ourselves as their risk-free solution, we dominated markets across healthcare, financial services, not-for-profit organizations, franchises, restaurants, and countless other affected industries. Entire clusters told their friends what they were doing and marched as one onto the cloud.

When There Is No Discontinuity

I imagine (at least hope) you're getting excited to find discontinuities for yourself if you haven't started already. But this chapter also begs the question: What if I find no actual discontinuities in the market I planned to pursue? Do I drop what I'm doing and pursue another set of hills?

You can try to pursue a set of hills without a discontinuity. You *may* find success there if you can solve a pain point no one else has solved and your solution can save the companies a ton of resources.

While this may occasionally work, you may not find much luck without a true discontinuity. Some companies may be motivated to switch, but it's possible none will be motivated. Plus, rather than winning large swaths of territory at once, you must painstakingly try to convince each account.

If the market you have been seeking is not experiencing a discontinuity, try expanding your sights and search for one that is. There is a principle I refer to as the **Law of Large Markets**. The law states that if you can't find a discontinuity, don't get hung up on it; a large market will *always* have other hills experiencing a discontinuity nearby. With the speed of Smart Conversations, you can pivot with very little skin off your back.

Pivoting in pursuit of the market shift can yield very high rewards. A brief example is the evolution of PayPal. PayPal grew out of a 1998 tech startup called Fieldlink. Fieldlink was created to develop security software for handheld devices (primarily PalmPilots, at the time). However, they soon found out PalmPilot already had their security needs met, and other enterprise customers didn't consider security as much of a problem. This would come in the future, but there was no discontinuity yet.

Eventually, they did come across a discontinuity for which they had the answer. As people began using the Internet for everything, there was a considerable growth in online marketplaces like eBay. But if the item had to be shipped, there was no way to make digital payments without handing over all your banking info to Mike's Bikes or some other user you had never met. Consumers had to discontinue the way they had made purchases and find a new way. Online marketplaces were also eager to find these new systems and maximize their profits.

PayPal eventually took off by tailoring its product to facilitate secure, digital payments between individuals. A partnership with eBay catapulted them into success.

All this to say: Market shifts are all around us. Even if the shifting market is not the one you originally envisioned, focusing your efforts there will put the wind at your back rather than swimming upstream.

Discovering a Discontinuity: Manual Versus ChatGPT

How do you discover whether a discontinuity is occurring for an industry or multiple industries? And how do you act when you discover one?

One might identify a discontinuity based on news announcements if that person can connect some dots. For example, when I heard the pandemic stay-at-home orders, I didn't need twenty customer interviews to tell me that droves of companies would need to switch to cloud software—and fast. Or if the government were to suddenly implement strict emissions standards, one could infer that companies across the automotive industry would be scrambling to rapidly redesign their vehicles.

That said, many discontinuities are not as widely publicized; they are often more niche, deeply affecting specific industries and subsets of those industries. For this reason, the primary manual way to find a discontinuity is through interviews. In the last stage, I described my methodology for interviewing customers (or potential customers). I included questions that would reveal key challenges and point to a discontinuity if one were present. Those questions were: "When you examine your key challenges and needs, which ones are most compelling to do now versus next year? What is the impact of not doing them?" If the interviewee describes a challenge that might put them out of business if they don't address it immediately, you've got yourself a discontinuity. Great! So then, how do you pursue it? First, you prepare a plan. Manually, this takes about three months, considering all that needs to be done: research, interviews, product integrations, pricing, competitive analysis, positioning, messaging … and more. Three months was once considered quick; the interviews alone could take up three months!

Hopefully, by the time you gather your plan, the market shift will still be relevant, and no one will have come to fill the need before you—but that isn't promised. One might prioritize speed only to get to market and find their slapdash plan is not landing. Conversely, one might prioritize quality and take the time to create an excellent strategy, only to find that someone has beaten them to it or the market shift has evolved, so their plan is no longer relevant.

The time it takes is already a significant liability of the manual way, but let's say you get a great plan together fast enough and can capture the business of the micro-vertical. Here's the following challenge: Because industries are all so connected, a domino effect occurs when one sector has to make a major change. That means where you find one discontinuity, you are likely to see more nearby.

Finding multiple market shifts at once is great news, right? Well, it is if you have the resources to capture it. However, we have already established that generalized plans with generic messaging sent out to multiple industries are ineffective. And if it generally takes three months or more to complete an effective, personalized plan, you can only deliver four quality plans a year, at most.

So even if you were to discover multiple market shifts, and even if you had the right product for all of them, you would likely not be able to capture them all. Thus, the manual method is limited, even when expertly done. You max out your bandwidth long before you can optimize on the market shift's full potential.

Of course, this is where Gen AI comes in to help. This help takes several different forms.

First, ChatGPT can help marketers by consolidating a list of the ICP's most pressing challenges and needs. These are gathered from any interviews you conducted and from what ChatGPT was able to scrape from publicly available information.

Second, ChatGPT can provide an objective lens to determine whether a pain point is an actual discontinuity or just a headache. This prevents teams from being misguided by "happy ears" moments when a marketing exec overestimates the customer's pain and invests too much in an approach the target audience is ultimately unready to accept.

Third, when you identify a genuine discontinuity affecting multiple industries, Smart Conversations can help you rapidly tailor not just *one* plan for *one* account but a whole *portfolio* of plans. You can target each business within the first hill, then immediately begin targeting each surrounding "hill" experiencing its unique version of the market shift.

Fourth, you don't have to bet everything on one horse. If you're relying on your manual capacity, you have to invest a lot of time and money into something that may fall through. The

ChatGPT native, on the other hand, can A/B/C/D test multiple related micro-vertical plans simultaneously to see which one gains the most traction quickly.

Lastly, on a more conceptual but very consequential note, finding and addressing discontinuities the manual way presupposes a static world. It's as if marketers expect all parties involved in the market shift to stay on hold for a few months until they can put together a plan and execute it. Addressing discontinuities through Smart Conversations allows for a dynamic world in which you can rapidly create a whole portfolio of plans and adapt them immediately to any new situation that may arise.

Overall, discovering discontinuities is critical to rapid success, where you can dominate not just one hill but a series of hills in twelve to eighteen months. Using Smart Conversations expands your bandwidth and expedites your strategic process so you can meet the market with deep precision and awe-inspiring scale.

The ChatGPT Smart Conversation: Discovering Discontinuities

The following Smart Conversation continues the conversation from the previous chapters. As a reminder, here is what we know from the conversation so far:

- I am chatting as a marketing leader searching for growth opportunities for Sage's product, Sage Intacct.
- ChatGPT helped me identify that family offices were a cluster among our existing customers that I could target further with minimal effort and high reward.
- Acting as a family office expert, ChatGPT helped me create an ICP complete with personas for each buying team member.

In this leg of the conversation, ChatGPT will help us identify if there are any true discontinuities in the cluster I am pursuing.

No additional uploads are required. However, you can upload new documents if you find new materials to describe customer pains or shifts you think might be discontinuous. The conversation is as follows.

PROMPT 1
Me: When you examine the key challenges and needs for the ICP, which ones are more compelling to address now than next year?

ChatGPT: In the family office software buying process, some pain points require immediate resolution (i.e., compelling reasons to act now), while others are important but can be addressed in the next budget cycle. Below is a breakdown of what forces urgency vs. what can be postponed.

"Do Now" – Urgent, Compelling Pain Points That Drive Immediate Action
(Why buy Sage Intacct today instead of waiting?)

Pain Point	Why It's Urgent	Major Requirement
Multi-Entity, Multi-Currency Complexity	Family offices with multiple trusts, LLCs, and partnerships struggle with manual consolidations and cannot get a real-time view of finances.	Automated multi-entity consolidations to avoid costly manual work and compliance risks
Regulatory & Compliance Risks (SEC, IRS, FATCA, GDPR, etc.)	New regulations (e.g., increased SEC scrutiny on private investments, tax rule changes) increase audit pressure.	Audit-ready reporting & real-time compliance monitoring
Manual Financial Reporting & Investor Statements	Family members and investors demand real-time, accurate reporting instead of waiting for manual reconciliations.	Automated financial reporting & dashboards
Cybersecurity Threats & Data Risks	Family offices are prime cyberattack targets. Legacy systems and spreadsheets pose security risks.	Cloud security, access controls, and automated backups
Rising Costs & Inefficiencies from Legacy Systems	On-premise or outdated systems require high maintenance costs, IT overhead, and manual work.	Cost-effective cloud migration to eliminate IT burden
Tax & Estate Planning Complexity	Tax deadlines and estate planning changes make accurate financial reporting critical.	Automated K-1 reporting & tax integrations

- **Compelling Event Triggers:**
  - New SEC/private investment regulations requiring detailed reporting
  - High-profile cyberattack on a peer firm
  - Family members demanding better transparency
  - Upcoming tax deadlines requiring accurate reporting
  - New CFO/Controller hired to "fix inefficiencies"

"Next Year" – Important, But Can Be Deferred
(Why would a family office delay implementation until the next budget cycle?)

Pain Point	Why It Can Wait	Major Requirement
AI & Predictive Analytics for Investment Performance	While AI can improve decision-making, family offices prioritize accounting accuracy first.	Advanced analytics & forecasting tools
Integration with Emerging Investment Platforms (e.g. Crypto, Private Credit, ESG Investments)	Offices investing in non-traditional assets need tracking, but it's a smaller pain point vs. compliance & automation.	APIs for seamless investment tracking
Automated Expense Management & Bill Pay	Manual bill pay is inefficient but is less urgent than financial reporting and compliance.	AP automation & bill pay
Full ERP-Level Customization	Some offices outgrow QuickBooks but don't yet need a fully customized ERP.	Scalable, modular ERP features
Outsourcing Accounting & Back-Office Functions	Many offices consider outsourcing instead of upgrading systems.	Cloud-based financial outsourcing options

- **Triggers for Next-Year Projects:**
  - New CIO looking for long-term investment analytics
  - Family office planning, ESG, or alternative investment expansions
  - Budget approval cycles delaying tech adoption

Key Takeaways for Sage Intacct Sales & Marketing Positioning

- **Urgent, "Do Now" Messaging Focus:**
  - Manual Financial Consolidation Pain: "Save 50+ hours per month with automation."
  - Regulatory & Compliance Risks: "Stay ahead of SEC, IRS, and tax rule changes."
  - Cybersecurity Threats: "Move sensitive data to a secure, cloud-based solution."
  - Rising IT & Legacy System Costs: "Eliminate expensive on-premise systems."

- **Next-Year Messaging for Future Consideration:**
  - AI analytics, emerging asset classes: "Build a future-proof investment tracking system."
  - Outsourcing, automation: "Scale your operations without adding headcount."
  - Bill pay, workflow tools: "Optimize financial efficiency with smarter automation."

PROMPT 2

Me: When you look at the compelling reasons for immediate action ("do now"), what is the impact of not doing them?

ChatGPT: For each compelling pain point, the impact of inaction can be severe—ranging from financial loss to regulatory non-compliance and reputational risk. Below is a breakdown of what happens if a family office doesn't address these urgent issues.

Compelling "Do Now" Issues & Consequences of Inaction

Pain Point	Impact of Not Acting	Who Feels the Pain Most?
Multi-Entity, Multi-Currency Complexity	- Financial Errors: Manual consolidation leads to misstatements, which can affect investment decisions. - Wasted Time: Teams spend 100+ hours per month on manual intercompany eliminations. - Cash Flow Blind Spots: Poor tracking delays capital calls and distributions.	CFO, Controller, Investment Manager
Regulatory & Compliance Risks (SEC, IRS, FATCA, GDPR, etc.)	- Regulatory Fines: Failure to comply with tax or SEC reporting can lead to six-figure penalties. - Failed Audits: Inaccurate records increase audit exposure. - Reputational Damage: Compliance failures hurt trust with family members, investors, and regulators.	CFO, Controller, Tax Advisors
Manual Financial Reporting & Investor Statements	- Slow Decision-Making: Family members and investment managers don't have real-time financial insights. - Poor Transparency: Lack of automated reporting creates frustration for UHNW families. - Errors in Performance Reporting: Incorrect calculations lead to bad investment decisions.	CFO, Family Office Principal, Investment Manager

Pain Point	Impact of Not Acting	Who Feels the Pain Most?
Cybersecurity Threats & Data Risks	- High Risk of Cyberattacks: Family offices are prime ransomware and phishing targets. - Data Breaches: Legacy systems lack encryption, MFA, and real-time monitoring. - Loss of Family Trust: Breached financial data damages family reputation and leads to lawsuits.	IT & Security Director, Family Office Principal
Rising Costs & Inefficiencies from Legacy Systems	- High IT Maintenance Costs: $100K+ annually wasted on outdated servers, support, and manual processes. - Staffing Issues: More headcount needed to manage workarounds instead of automation. - Lack of Modern Integrations: Old systems don't connect with banks, investment platforms, or AI analytics.	CFO, Controller, IT Director
Tax & Estate Planning Complexity	- Missed Tax Deadlines: Late K-1s and IRS filings result in penalties. - Estate Disputes: Inaccurate tracking leads to conflicts over inheritance and trust distributions. - Increased Legal & Accounting Fees: More time spent fixing issues = higher costs.	Tax Advisors, CFO, Family Office Principal

Summary: Why Family Offices Must Act Now

- Financial Impact: Errors & inefficiencies waste hundreds of thousands per year.
- Regulatory Risks: SEC, IRS, or GDPR fines can damage reputation & trust.
- Time Loss: Controllers & CFOs spend weeks on manual work that could be automated.
- Security Threats: Cyberattacks can expose confidential family financial data.
- Family Trust Issues: Poor reporting undermines confidence in the office's management.

PROMPT 3

Me: What is the discontinuity or market shift driving these "do now" pains?

ChatGPT: The Discontinuity Driving "Do Now" Pains in Family Offices

A discontinuity is a fundamental market shift or external pressure that forces organizations to rethink the status quo. For family offices, the "do now" pains are driven by multiple disruptive forces that make inaction too risky.

The Four Key Discontinuities Driving Urgency

- **Discontinuity #1: New Regulatory Pressures & Tax Scrutiny (Compliance Shock)**
  - **What's Changing?**
    - SEC & IRS enforcement is tightening on alternative assets, tax filings, and investment transparency.
    - Private fund rule changes increase reporting burdens for family offices investing in private equity, hedge funds, and real estate.

- Global tax reporting (FATCA, CRS, OECD BEPS rules) demand greater financial transparency.
  - **Why Is This Urgent?**
    - Penalties for non-compliance are increasing.
    - Audits are rising, and outdated financial systems create high audit risks.
    - Families are demanding transparency, and poor reporting creates disputes.
  - **Impact of Inaction:**
    - Heavy regulatory fines ($100K+ per violation)
    - Increased audit scrutiny & legal risks
    - Loss of tax-efficient wealth structures
  - **How Sage Intacct Solves It:**
    - Automated GAAP & IFRS compliance
    - Pre-built tax & audit reports
    - Secure data storage for global reporting

- **Discontinuity #2: Shift from Legacy On-Premise to Cloud (Tech Modernization Shock)**
  - **What's Changing?**
    - Legacy on-premise financial systems are being phased out, leaving offices with unsupported or costly IT burdens.
    - Family offices increasingly expect real-time access to financial data, not batch processing or manual spreadsheets.
    - Cybersecurity threats have made cloud adoption essential for risk mitigation.
  - **Why Is This Urgent?**
    - IT costs for maintaining legacy systems are rising.
    - Vendors are discontinuing support for outdated financial platforms.

- Family offices are prime cyberattack targets, and old systems are vulnerable.
  - o **Impact of Inaction:**
    - Costly manual workarounds and IT maintenance fees ($100K+ per year)
    - Increased risk of financial data breaches
    - Limited ability to scale or integrate with modern investment platforms
  - o **How Sage Intacct Solves It:**
    - Fully cloud-based, reducing IT overhead
    - Bank-level security & encryption
    - API-driven integrations with wealth management platforms

- **Discontinuity #3: Rising Complexity of family office Investments (Alternative Asset Shock)**
  - o **What's Changing?**
    - Family offices are shifting from traditional stock/bond portfolios to complex alternatives (private equity, venture capital, real estate, hedge funds).
    - Waterfall calculations, capital calls, and carried interest tracking require advanced financial tools.
    - More multi-entity, cross-border structures demand automated consolidation.
  - o **Why Is Urgent?**
    - Legacy systems weren't designed for modern alternative asset accounting.
    - Investment teams can't get real-time insights into fund performance.
    - Manual tracking leads to costly errors in tax filings and distributions.

- o **Impact of Inaction:**
  - Missed capital calls, leading to penalties
  - Poor financial visibility for investment decisions
  - Expensive external consultants to fill reporting gaps
- o **How Sage Intacct Solves It:**
  - Automated waterfall & intercompany eliminations
  - Real-time dashboards for investment performance
  - Multi-entity consolidation with alternative asset tracking

- **Discontinuity #4: Increasing Demand for Transparency & Governance (Trust Shock)**
  - o **What Is Urgent?**
    - Family members are questioning opaque reporting from legacy systems.
    - Mismanagement risks family disputes and potential lawsuits.
    - Philanthropy & ESG goals require tracking and auditability.
  - o **Impact of Inaction:**
    - Loss of trust in family office leadership
    - Weaker decision-making from outdated reporting
    - Potential family governance conflicts
  - o **How Sage Intacct Solves It:**
    - Customizable dashboards for family members
    - Audit-ready financials to build trust
    - Secure collaboration & access controls

Summary: Why Family Offices Must Act Now

Discontinuity	What's Changing?	Urgency Level	Sage Intacct's Advantage
Regulatory Shock	Stricter SEC, IRS, and global tax rules	Critical	Pre-built compliance & audit tools
Tech Modernization	Legacy on-premise systems failing	Critical	Fully cloud-native, reducing IT costs
Alternative Asset Complexity	More investments in private equity & hedge funds	High	Automated multi-entity, investment tracking
Transparency & Trust Issues	Next-gen families demanding more visibility	High	Real-time dashboards & secure access

Key Message for Family Office Buyers:
"The family office landscape has fundamentally changed. Old financial systems are no longer secure, compliant, or efficient. The cost of doing nothing is too high—whether it's financial penalties, cyber risks, or poor investment decisions. Sage Intacct helps you stay ahead of these disruptions with a modern, secure, and automated financial platform."

Conversation Highlights

In minutes, ChatGPT discovered which pain points might be career-threatening to the ICP if they don't act fast. Those were: 1) regulatory and tax pressures, 2) shift to the cloud, 3) rising complexity of family office investments, and 4) increasing demand for transparency. This confirms what we learned through the buyer personas, and it gives more color to what is driving those pains: Stricter regulations, failing legacy systems, trends toward more diverse investments, and an increasing demand for transparency from next-gen family members.

One of the most remarkable parts of this conversation is when ChatGPT explains the impact of not acting, and it explains *why* inaction will impact companies in the ways described. This takes fantastic knowledge of an industry. In the past, we couldn't have gotten this depth of understanding without interviewing at least twenty customers and manually analyzing the common pain points (think: all my pages of customer interviews spread across a string of desks).

When I did this manual interview process, the primary discontinuity I discovered was the trend toward alternative asset complexity. Specifically, there was a big push to invest in real estate at the time—everything from office buildings to orchards—which presented overwhelming challenges for the team to report on and consolidate. While ChatGPT's response included this discontinuity I found, it also identified three more than I had seen—and it evaluated the current landscape without me needing to interview fifty people all over again.

Key Output for Step 3

After this conversation about your ideal customer's challenges, you should have:

- A concise summary of your ICP's most demanding challenges and needs
- A list of which challenges are genuine discontinuities to act on
- Further clarity on whether to:
  - Pursue: Your micro-vertical has a true discontinuity and is motivated to become your customer.
  - Ponder: Do further research to understand more deeply whether there is a discontinuity and/or if you have the solution.

    o   Pivot: Even if you have what the customer needs, there is no motivation to make a change; you have qualified out this micro-vertical and can now explore others.

CHAPTER 6
Learning the Battle Landscape

At this point, you have your set of hills to target. Through Smart Conversations paired with your own experience, you have crafted an ICP to understand the people on those hills deeply. And now, you've also discovered which of your ideal customers' pains demand immediate action. With this preparation, you have your sights set on an excellent target. You're ready to charge!

... But wait! As you start moving in, you realize you have some competition. Who is your competition? Luckily, it's not the giants with machine guns! By foregoing the heavily defended hill and pursuing the medium-sized hills, you dodged the most brutal competition that would have caused you the most casualties.

That said, there are still a couple of other players you'll need to contend with. This phase is about discovering who you are competing against—and what allies you may need to partner with to win the battle.

Sizing Up the Competition

The first player you must face is the "legacy competitor." A **legacy competitor** is a company that has been operating in a market for a long time with an established brand and customer base. Also known as an "old-world competitor," they are the incumbent. They most likely have some highly specialized functionality that the customer cannot find anywhere else. They are likely ubiquitous in the micro-vertical community.

While taking on a company so deeply ingrained in the community may sound intimidating, you have key advantages to wield. Just because they are ubiquitous does not mean the customers on the hills are happy. The old guard has been living fat and lazy, knowing their customers have no alternative. Not only do they often gouge their customers with their pricing, but their systems are also typically archaic. They have had no motivation to innovate or keep up with the changing landscape.

To them, you are a "new-world competitor." A **new-world competitor** is a newer company on the market offering a fresh perspective or innovative product/service that disrupts the existing landscape. Typically, these companies leverage emerging technologies and changes in consumer behavior.

As a new-world competitor, you can easily overtake the giant but dwindling dinosaur if you focus on the right tactics. You *don't* want to focus on comparing your product to theirs, feature set versus feature set. If you present that to customers, you will likely lose. Why? Because this highlights the legacy competitor's strengths. They have spent years or decades in this market; they have the specialized feature set that the customer needs and understand it far better than you, the newbie.

Your ticket to victory is pitting old-world problems against new-world solutions. Let me give you an example from one of my favorite customer stories.

When I worked as CMO for Intacct (before Sage bought it), I was investigating the cluster of family offices. In doing so, I set up a conversation to get to know one of our customers, Gary.

Gary was the CFO of a family office in Naples, Florida. It was 2017, and he had signed on with Intacct a year or so earlier.

I asked him on a call one day, "Gary, what were you using for your accounting software before you switched to Intacct?"

"Oh," he chuckled. "Nothing fancy, that's for sure. At our little office on the coast, we had a room—more like a walk-in closet—full of servers running the Microsoft accounting system. I started hearing about the cloud and knew that was probably the way to go, but switching over would have been a big undertaking. And our old bones had always gotten the job done just fine until 2014. That was when we found you guys."

"And what led you to switch in 2014?" I asked. "I recall it had to do with the hurricanes. Can you tell me more?"

"Oh boy," Gary sighed. "2014 was a tough year for us. It was a record year with four hurricanes back to back. Of course, we'd had some minor flooding here and there, and we have protections for that. But this was madness, and there was nothing we could do. We had to leave all our computers and data on-premises."

"Wow." I exhaled. "That must have been terrifying on multiple levels. What did you do?"

Gary responded, "Well, luckily, one guy had a backup of our data on a *tape* at his house. Talk about old school, but thank god for it. He was able to grab it before he evacuated. But by that time, all our employees were scattered, and it took us *weeks* to get back up and running again. In the meantime, business was at a total standstill."

After a beat, he went on. "After all that, we knew there was no going back to the old way. With the way things are going, we knew that was not going to be the last hurricane, and we could not let that happen again. We practically ran into the salesman's arms when Intacct reached out to us about getting set up on the cloud."

I smiled. "I'm so glad we found you at just the right time. And I know Florida did just get hit with another bad hurricane. How did you all fare?"

"Ian," he said emphatically, "Intacct has been the best decision we ever made. When hurricane Irma hit, I took my laptop and hopped on a plane with my family to Atlanta. We were up and running again in a few hours. Absolute night and day difference. The damage overall was even worse than the last time, but our company operations were relatively unaffected. Our employees moved to safety and had everything they needed from wherever they were. We can't sing your praises enough!"

Stories like this fill me with pride, but they also illustrate the old-world versus new-world point: Victory over the legacy player can be tough if there is no discontinuity. Without the storm, it may have taken several more years before they finally worked up the motivation to update to a better system. Gary and his team simply could not bring themselves to perform the "heart surgery" required to transition from the Microsoft legacy system to the cloud.

Yet after the discontinuity brought by the hurricane, the old dinosaur didn't stand a chance. When a market shift occurs and the customer is forced to make a change, they will rarely, if ever, choose to go back to the same outdated systems that failed them.

Pitching to Gary, we didn't need to sell him on all our bells and whistles. Our pitch was built on the fact that switching to the cloud would protect them well into the future. They signed on without a second thought and became some of our biggest fans.

Besides the legacy systems, the other players you'll face in pursuit of the hills are other new-world competitors. These are companies like yours with the advantage of modern technology and a fresh perspective on customer behavior. Against these companies, you must not just prove that you can fix the pain with new-world solutions. You must also prove that you can do better than the next guy.

An example of new-world competitors would be Netflix versus HBO Max in the modern streaming market or Tesla versus Rivian in electric car manufacturing. For Sage, it would be another company with cloud accounting software (like NetSuite or Microsoft). Against these competitors, we had to show we had a better solution to their problem than even other new-world systems.

In other words, we have already discovered "Why switch?" (the customer has a problem in their system) and "Why now?" (the problem is urgent), but we need to answer the question, "Why me and not them?" If you're standing there with a bucket of water, and your new-world competitor is standing beside you with a fire extinguisher, can't both solve their problem? Why should they choose you over the other?

Effective Competitive Analysis

Most companies know they must perform **competitive analysis** before charging into a market. Competitive analysis is the process of researching how complex the competitive landscape will be and what partners they may need to work with to achieve victory.

That said, competitive analysis is typically done poorly, even in companies with hundreds of millions of dollars in annual recurring revenue. I cannot count how many PowerPoint presentations I have sat through on the subject. It's always the same: a set of "Feature, Function, Benefit" slides with Harvey Balls trying desperately to prove some differentiation between us and the competition. Typically, it is in no way intuitively obvious why one product is better.

Effective competitive analysis does not just consider product-to-product comparison. It considers the larger competitive landscape as a whole, including the following questions:

- Is there a legacy competitor? If so, who?
- Is there a discontinuity driving customers away from the legacy competitor?
- Does our standard out-of-the-box product fix the problem caused by the discontinuity and fix it well?
- Has another new-world competitor already won this market?
- If not, are there any new-world competitors trying to win the market?
- Is our new-world competitor weak in the area of the problem?
- Can the competition easily copy or outdo our greatest strengths?
- Who might we need to partner with to win the battle?
- Where are we already winning, why are we winning, and who do we beat most often?

I want to emphasize points 3 and 6: Does my product fix the problem caused by the discontinuity, and is the competitor weak in this area? This is crucial. I can be better than my competitor in a dozen ways, but if I am not better than them in the area of the customer's burning need, I will not win.

Imagine your child is stuck on the top of a hill, and you cannot traverse on foot to get to them. One person offers you a Ferrari; another offers you a Land Rover. The Ferrari is faster and more elegant, and it outmatches the Land Rover in terms of raw road performance. But you couldn't care less. Your child is stuck. You say, "Can the Ferrari get me up this rocky hill to get my kid? No? Then get out of my way!" You take the Land Rover, which is capable of climbing rough terrain and bringing your kid to safety. You choose the strongest option in the area of your most urgent need.

Let's say you and your competitor both have viable solutions. You can try to differentiate yourself by having a better product, and you should, of course, try to make the best product you can. However, this form of differentiation *alone* is challenging to sustain. Your product might be better today, but tomorrow, your competitor will develop a new feature, and theirs will be better. You'll work to surpass them again. It feels like a game of leapfrog. It's easy to get caught up in over-focusing on feature after feature, trying desperately to stay ahead. Of course, the customer cares about the product, but this is not always where meaningful competitive gains are made.

Strong and *sustainable* differentiation can come in many other forms, including the following:

- Deeper audience understanding
  - You better understand the target market's needs and know how to speak their language more fluently than your other new-world competitors.
- Pre-existing customer base
  - You already have a cluster of customers from this market you can point to for successful case studies. Prospects are more likely to trust you over the competition if you already have a good track record in their community. You pose less of a risk than your untested competitor.

- Critical partnerships
  - You recognize that your customers will have needs related to your product or that help them use your product better. If you cannot serve these needs, you collaborate with companies that have complementary strengths.
- Whole product relationship
  - You recognize that you are not just selling a physical product but all aspects of the customer's experience while using that product. In your offer, you include additional services, customer support, branding, and other elements that contribute to the overall value and usability of the product straight out of the box (like an iPhone with a charging cord).

Sometimes, your competitor can easily replicate your newest feature, playing the continuous game of product leapfrog with you. However, it's much more difficult for them to replicate your deep understanding without doing the work themselves. They can't replicate your prior credibility without taking time to build their own. They can't easily replicate your key partnerships, as it takes time to build trust, and relationships can be exclusive. They can't replicate your whole product relationship without having the same business and product partners and integrations. Each of these is very difficult to copy.

Differentiating factors like these give customers a compelling reason to buy your product over another that could also address their need.

The Battle Landscape: Manual Versus ChatGPT

Again, while this intensive competitive analysis is differentiating, it is also laborious.

On one side of your battle landscape, you have legacy competitors. Each micro-vertical has these, but they're tough to research because it's likely you don't really understand them, know the right questions to ask, or know the terms to use. Asking the right questions requires understanding the whole industry and its dynamics.

Not only that, but research on legacy competitors is also tedious because they may have very little info about themselves on the web. Think about it: They have had a consistent customer base for generations and have not had to put much work into marketing themselves. Whatever they do have on their website may be very basic or outdated, with poor SEO, hidden ten pages into the search results, with a title that doesn't clearly tell you what the contents even contain.

Manually researching your new-world competitor's strengths and weaknesses is tricky for different reasons. They may be more familiar and visible online (like Microsoft or NetSuite). However, you need to peer deeply into their product to understand how strong they are in the area of the discontinuity. You likely don't have inside access to use the product itself, and the details you're looking for may be too specific for them to spell out on their website. You'd likely need to conduct interviews with customers who have used their product previously or look at comparison sites to gain deeper insight about its weaknesses in a particular area. It is time-consuming to dig down to the information you need.

Smart Conversations bypass nearly all (if not all) of these obstacles. If you ask ChatGPT a precise question, it will give you a precise answer. When you ask about your competitor, it will search the recesses of the Internet in a way you do not have time for, and it will scrape information from sources you didn't know existed. Rather than sifting through loads of articles across pages of search results, ChatGPT will give you a tailor-made article consolidating information from various sources.

The ChatGPT Smart Conversation
PART 1: Competitive Analysis

The following Smart Conversation continues the conversation from the previous chapters. As a reminder, here is what we know from the conversation so far:

- I am chatting as a marketing leader searching for growth opportunities for Sage's product, Sage Intacct.
- ChatGPT helped me identify that family offices were a cluster among our existing customers I could target further.
- Acting as a family office expert, ChatGPT helped me create an ICP.
- Acting as a family office expert, ChatGPT has told me the most prominent discontinuities family offices are facing: 1) regulatory and tax pressures, 2) shift to the cloud, 3) rising complexity of family office investments, and 4) increasing demand for transparency.

Before we begin, I want to let you know that this conversation will be divided into two parts. The first part will focus on competitive analysis. The second part will combine what we learn from competitive analysis with what we learned about discontinuities in the last chapter. This way, our insights from each chapter will build on one another, creating an ever-more-practical battle strategy. Let's begin.

PROMPT 1

Me: Who are the legacy on-premises family office specialists in the mid-market of 20 to 999 employees that compete against the product, Sage Intacct?

ChatGPT:
In the mid-market family office space, Sage Intacct competes primarily against legacy, on-premises financial management

solutions that have traditionally dominated the space. These vendors offer deep multi-entity, multi-currency, and partnership accounting capabilities but often lack modern cloud scalability, automation, and AI-driven insights.

Key Legacy On-Premises Family Office Software Competitors (Mid-Market)

- **FIS Investran**
  - **Strengths:** Deep alternative asset accounting, investor reporting, waterfall calculations, and fund administration features.
  - **Weaknesses:** Complex implementation, expensive to maintain, lacks cloud-native automation, and the user experience is outdated.
  - **Typical Users:** PE-backed family offices, private equity firms, and fund administrators managing alternative investments.

- **SS&C Geneva**
  - **Strengths:** Strong investment accounting, portfolio consolidation, performance reporting, and reconciliation.
  - **Weaknesses:** Designed for hedge funds, lacks modern cloud capabilities, and requires expensive IT overhead.
  - **Typical Users:** Investment-heavy family offices and multi-family offices managing hedge funds and complex assets.

- **Eton Solutions**
  - **Strengths:** Built specifically for single and multi-family offices, includes entity management and governance features.
  - **Weaknesses:** On-premises/hosted model, slow innovation, expensive implementations.
  - **Typical Users:** Large, sophisticated family offices with in-house finance teams.

- **Asset Vantage**
  - **Strengths:** Strong reporting for multi-asset portfolios, partnership accounting, and alternative investment tracking.
  - **Weaknesses:** Primarily hosted/on-premises, lacks the broader ecosystem and automation of true cloud platforms.
  - **Typical Users:** UHNW family offices focused on complex investment portfolios.
- **Addepar (Hybrid, but legacy roots)**
  - **Strengths:** Excellent portfolio performance tracking and data aggregation.
  - **Weaknesses:** Not a full accounting suite, often used alongside other legacy accounting systems.
  - **Typical Users:** Family offices with a heavy focus on investment reporting but needing a separate general ledger.

Where Sage Intacct Wins vs. Legacy Products

- **Cloud-Native:** No IT burden, real-time access, and modern API integrations.
- **Multi-Entity & Multi-Currency:** Consolidation and real-time financial insights across complex structures.
- **Automated Workflows:** AI-driven automation and continuous close capabilities.
- **Scalability:** Suitable for single-family, multi-family, and hybrid investment-focused offices.
- **Open Ecosystem:** Seamless integration with investment management, tax, and estate planning tools.

ChatGPT has done an excellent job rounding up the legacy competitors, which are very niche and would have taken laborious research to find on the web. That said, I don't opt for more information on legacy competition here because I have gathered from previous conversations that a discontinuity is driving customers away from these legacy options. I want to focus on my new-world competitors, where the real battle will take place.

PROMPT 2
Me: You are now an expert in the cloud financial space, having been an analyst for over 20 years

Note that I am now changing ChatGPT's persona. In previous chapters, I told it to answer me as an expert in the family office space to give me insider knowledge on my target customer. But now, I want it to respond with the expertise of someone in my field who understands how cloud-based accounting works and who I'll compete against.

PROMPT 3
Me: Can you tell me how cloud-based financial solutions address the key discontinuities in the family office space?[10]

---

[10] ChatGPT's response to this question was quite long to include in this book, so I also asked it to summarize its response. What's included here is the summary, which still includes all substantial details.

ChatGPT: Family offices face increasing structural, regulatory, and technological disruptions that make legacy financial systems unsustainable. Cloud-based financial solutions like Sage Intacct address these challenges by improving automation, security, and compliance. Below is an analysis of how cloud financials solve the four major discontinuities affecting family offices today.

Discontinuity #1: Regulatory & Compliance Challenges

- **What's Changing?**
  - Stricter SEC & IRS oversight on alternative investments, trusts, and tax structures
  - Global tax transparency (FATCA, CRS, OECD BEPS) is increasing
  - Complex multi-entity reporting and K-1 distributions require automation
- **Risk of Not Adapting:**
  - Regulatory fines ($100 K+ per violation)
  - Increased audit exposure and legal risks
  - Loss of trust from family members due to financial mismanagement
- **How Cloud Financials Solve This:**
  - Automated Compliance & Tax Reporting—Prebuilt audit-ready reports for SEC, IRS, and FATCA compliance
  - Secure, Role-Based Access Controls—Ensures data protection and proper governance
  - Multi-Jurisdiction Tax Support—Automated tax calculations & K-1 distributions

Cloud financials ensure compliance, reduce audit exposure, and provide financial transparency.

Discontinuity #2: Legacy On-Premise to Cloud Transition
- **What's Changing?**
  - Legacy accounting systems (FIS Investran, SS&C Geneva, QuickBooks Enterprise) are outdated
  - On-premise ERP solutions require heavy IT maintenance
  - Family offices need real-time financial visibility
- **Risk of Not Adapting:**
  - High IT costs ($100K+/year) for maintaining outdated systems
  - Lack of scalability as family structures grow
  - Cybersecurity vulnerabilities exposing sensitive data
- **How Cloud Financials Solve This:**
  - 100% Cloud-Native, No IT Overhead—No servers to maintain, automatic compliance updates
  - Real-Time Financial Visibility—Instant multi-entity rollups & live dashboards
  - Enterprise-Grade Cybersecurity—SOC 2, ISO 27001, and MFA protections

Cloud-based solutions eliminate IT burden, improve security, and enable real-time decision-making.

Discontinuity #3: Alternative Asset Complexity & Multi-Entity Growth
- **What's Changing?**
  - Family offices are investing in private equity, hedge funds, and real estate.
  - Capital calls, waterfall distributions, and carried interest tracking require automation.
  - Multi-entity structures require seamless financial consolidation.
- **Risk of Not Adapting:**
  - Errors in investment allocations → Financial losses.

- o Missed capital calls → Lost investment opportunities.
- o Manual consolidations → Inefficient & costly reporting cycles.
- **How Cloud Financials Solve This:**
  - o Automated Multi-Entity Accounting—Consolidates 100+ trusts, LLCs, partnerships
  - o Investment & Fund Accounting—Automates capital calls, carried interest, and distributions
  - o Portfolio & NAV Reporting in Real Time—Custom dashboards for family principals & CIOs

Cloud platforms simplify investment tracking, automate fund structures, and reduce reporting inefficiencies.

Discontinuity #4: Transparency & Governance Demands from Next-Gen Heirs

- **What's Changing?**
  - o Younger family members demand greater financial transparency
  - o Stronger governance models are becoming a requirement
  - o Philanthropy, ESG, and impact investing need better tracking
- **Risk of Not Adapting:**
  - o Loss of family trust: Next-gen disengagement from wealth management.
  - o Weak financial controls: Estate disputes & mismanagement.
  - o Inability to track impact investing: Lack of philanthropic accountability.
- **How Cloud Financials Solve This:**
  - o Customizable Dashboards for Family Members—Role-based access ensures secure transparency
  - o Audit-Ready Governance & Risk Controls—Automated audit logs & compliance workflows

- o Philanthropy & ESG Reporting—Automated donation tracking & impact investing reports

Cloud financials modernize governance, ensure generational wealth sustainability, and enhance financial transparency.

In the previous chapter, ChatGPT helped us identify the top four market shifts driving our target customers to act. In the response above, it just outlined exactly why they need our type of product to solve their most urgent pains created by the discontinuity. Next, we want to know who else will be competing with us to provide them with a new-world solution.

PROMPT 4

Me: Who are the top 3 major cloud financial SaaS players in the mid-market of 20 to 999 employees?

ChatGPT: The top three cloud financial SaaS players in the mid-market (20 to 999 employees) are:

1. **Sage Intacct**
   - **Focus**: Best-in-class **core financials** and accounting software
   - **Strengths**:
     - o **Multi-Entity Consolidation**: Exceptional at consolidating across multiple entities, currencies, and dimensions
     - o **Advanced Reporting and Dashboards**: Customizable dashboards for real-time visibility into KPIs
     - o **Ease of Use**: Financially focused, user-friendly platform tailored for mid-market businesses

- **Industries**: Financial services, SaaS, nonprofits, real estate, healthcare, and family offices
- **Position**: The go-to solution for organizations prioritizing **financial management** over a full ERP suite
- **Why It Stands Out**: Sage Intacct's deep financial capabilities make it ideal for multi-entity organizations and businesses requiring advanced reporting.

2. Oracle NetSuite

- **Focus**: A comprehensive **ERP suite** with integrated financials, inventory, and CRM
- **Strengths**:
  - **Broad ERP Functionality**: Combines financials with supply chain management, e-commerce, and CRM
  - **Multi-Currency, Multi-Entity**: Robust support for global operations and complex ownership structures
  - **Scalability**: Designed to grow with businesses as they expand in size and complexity
- **Industries**: Professional services, retail, manufacturing, SaaS, wholesale distribution
- **Position**: A dominant choice for businesses seeking an all-in-one ERP system
- **Why It Stands Out**: NetSuite's all-encompassing suite offers seamless integration of financials with other operational functions.

3. Microsoft Dynamics 365 Business Central

- **Focus**: ERP and **financial management** for mid-sized businesses
- **Strengths**:
  - **Integration with Microsoft Ecosystem**: Works seamlessly with Microsoft tools like Office 365, Power BI, and Azure
  - **Modular Approach**: Flexible, scalable ERP designed for customization

- o **Affordability**: Cost-effective for organizations transitioning from legacy systems like QuickBooks
- **Industries**: Professional services, manufacturing, distribution, nonprofits
- **Position**: A strong alternative for mid-market businesses already invested in Microsoft technologies
- **Why It Stands Out**: Combines familiar tools and interfaces with robust financial capabilities

Comparison

Vendor	Focus	Strengths	Best For
Sage Intacct	Core financials	Advanced reporting, multi-entity focus	Financially driven organizations
NetSuite	Full ERP suite	Integrated financials + operations	Growing businesses needing ERP
Dynamics 365	Financials and ERP	Microsoft ecosystem integration	Microsoft-focused organizations

Summary
- **Sage Intacct**: Best for mid-market organizations needing financial excellence without ERP complexity
- **Oracle NetSuite**: Ideal for businesses requiring a comprehensive ERP suite with integrated operational tools
- **Microsoft Dynamics 365 Business Central**: Great for mid-market firms leveraging the Microsoft ecosystem for modular ERP solutions

These three platforms lead the mid-market cloud financial space by catering to diverse organizational needs and growth trajectories.

PROMPT 5

Me: What product is the primary competitor for Sage Intacct?

ChatGPT: The primary competitor for Sage Intacct in the mid-market financial management space is Oracle NetSuite.

Why Oracle NetSuite is the Primary Competitor
- **Market Position**
  - o **NetSuite**: Positioned as a cloud ERP solution that offers integrated financials, ERP, CRM, and e-commerce
  - o **Sage Intacct**: Specializes in core financial management with strong multi-entity and dimensional reporting, tailored for mid-sized businesses

While both target the mid-market, NetSuite's broader suite appeals to businesses seeking end-to-end ERP capabilities, whereas Sage Intacct's depth in financial management is its primary strength.

- **Key Product Differentiators**

Feature/Focus	Sage Intacct	Oracle NetSuite
Core Strength	Financial management and reporting	Broad ERP with integrated financials
Multi-Entity Consolidation	Best-in-class for complex consolidations	Strong, but less robust for deep financials
Customizability	Highly flexible dimensions and dashboards	Full-suite customization capabilities
Ease of Use	Financials-focused, user-friendly	Steeper learning curve for ERP modules
Industries Served	Financial services, family offices, SaaS	Services, wholesale, manufacturing, SaaS
Implementation Speed	Faster implementation (financials only)	Longer implementation (broader ERP)
Pricing	Modular, financials-first pricing	Higher cost due to full-suite offerings

- **Areas of Competition**
  - **Financial Management**: NetSuite offers financials as part of its suite, but Sage Intacct often outperforms in multi-entity consolidations, dimensional reporting, and advanced analytics for financial teams.
  - **ERP Functionality**: NetSuite provides inventory management, CRM, procurement, and e-commerce within a single platform, while Sage Intacct relies on third-party partnerships for those capabilities.
  - **Industry Focus**:
    - **Sage Intacct** excels in financial services, family offices, SaaS, and professional services.
    - **NetSuite** serves a broader range of industries, including wholesale distribution, manufacturing, and retail.

- **Competitive Scenarios**
  - **Companies Requiring ERP Features**: Businesses needing integrated inventory, CRM, and e-commerce alongside financials often choose **NetSuite**.
  - **Financial Services and Complex Multi-Entity Organizations**: Sage Intacct is preferred when deep **financial reporting**, real-time consolidation, and scalability across entities are critical.
  - **Growth-Stage Businesses**: NetSuite's "ERP suite" offering may appeal to companies anticipating rapid growth, while Sage Intacct provides a more focused and modular path for businesses centered on financial excellence.
- **Emerging Competitors** While NetSuite is the primary competitor, other platforms are also gaining traction in the mid-market:
  - **Microsoft Dynamics 365 Business Central**: Strong choice for mid-sized businesses already invested in the Microsoft ecosystem.
  - **Acumatica**: Cloud-based ERP with strong flexibility and industry-specific solutions (construction, manufacturing).
  - **FinancialForce**: Niche player for **professional services** firms leveraging Salesforce.

Summary

- **Oracle NetSuite** is Sage Intacct's primary competitor due to its **broad ERP suite**, strong market presence, and appeal to mid-market businesses seeking a single platform.
- **Sage Intacct** maintains a competitive edge for organizations prioritizing **financial management**, advanced reporting, and multi-entity consolidations, especially in **financial services, SaaS, and family offices**.

By focusing on **best-in-class financials** and fostering strong integrations with complementary SaaS solutions, Sage Intacct differentiates itself from Oracle NetSuite's broader (but sometimes less specialized) ERP suite.

PROMPT 6
Me: For Sage Intacct to win against its competitors, what are the top five SaaS applications it needs, and what partners will those require?

ChatGPT: To win against comprehensive ERP suites like Oracle NetSuite or Microsoft Dynamics 365, Sage Intacct must focus on strategic SaaS applications that address critical operational needs while complementing its strengths in core financial management. Below are the top 5 SaaS categories and recommended partners for Sage Intacct:

1. **Financial Planning and Analysis (FP&A)**
   - **Importance**:
     - o Provides advanced budgeting, forecasting, and scenario planning to enable data-driven decision-making.
     - o Enhances Sage Intacct's core financial reporting with forward-looking analytics.
   - **Recommended Partners**:
     - o **Planful**: Known for intuitive budgeting and forecasting tailored to mid-market needs.
     - o **Adaptive Insights (Workday)**: Offers robust modeling and scenario planning for scaling businesses.
     - o **Vena Solutions**: Combines FP&A functionality with seamless Excel integration.
     - o **Jirav**: Simplified forecasting and planning for mid-sized organizations.

2. **Accounts Payable (AP) Automation**
   - **Importance**:
     - o Streamlines invoice processing, approvals, and vendor payments, reducing manual workloads and errors.
     - o Strengthens Sage Intacct's AP capabilities by automating workflows and improving efficiency.
   - **Recommended Partners**:
     - o **Bill.com**: Deep integration with Sage Intacct; automates invoice management and payments.
     - o **Tipalti**: Global AP solution with payment automation and compliance support.
     - o **AvidXchange**: Focused on AP automation and invoice processing for mid-sized businesses.

3. **Subscription Billing and Revenue Management**
   - **Importance**:
     - o Supports subscription-based revenue models, a growing need for SaaS and services businesses.
     - o Ensures compliance with ASC 606 and IFRS 15 revenue recognition standards.
   - **Recommended Partners**:
     - o **Zuora**: Industry leader in subscription billing and revenue automation.
     - o **SaaSOptics (Maxio)**: Tailored for SaaS companies; offers robust revenue recognition and analytics.
     - o **Chargebee**: Simple, scalable subscription billing for growing businesses.

4. **Procurement and Spend Management**
   - **Importance**:

- o Improves cost control and procurement workflows by streamlining purchasing, approvals, and vendor management.
- o Provides visibility into spending patterns, enhancing financial governance.
- **Recommended Partners**:
  - o **Coupa**: Comprehensive spend management solution with procurement automation.
  - o **Procurify**: Easy-to-use procurement and spend management for mid-sized organizations.
  - o **Tipalti Approve**: Focused on automating procurement workflows and integrating with payment systems.

5. **Human Capital Management (HCM) and Payroll**
- **Importance**:
  - o Addresses payroll, time tracking, and employee management needs to provide a holistic view of HR and financial data.
  - o Complements Sage Intacct's financial capabilities by integrating workforce management.
- **Recommended Partners**:
  - o **ADP**: Leading payroll and HR provider with integrations for seamless financial reporting.
  - o **Paylocity**: Payroll and HR software tailored for mid-market organizations.
  - o **Workforce Go!**: Specifically designed to integrate Sage Intacct with payroll and HCM tools.

Summary of Top Categories and Partners

Category	Importance	Recommended Partners
Financial Planning (FP&A)	Budgeting, forecasting	Planful, Adaptive Insights, Vena, Jirav
AP Automation	Streamlined vendor payments	Bill.com, Tipalti, AvidXchange
Subscription Billing	Recurring revenue models	Zuora, SaaSOptics, Chargebee
Procurement/Spend Mgmt	Cost control and procurement	Coupa, Procurify, Tipalti, Approve
HCM Payroll	Employee payroll and management	ADP, Paylocity, Workforce Go!

- **Strategic Approach**
  - **Focus on Financial Excellence**: Strengthen Sage Intacct's **financial management leadership** by integrating best-in-class SaaS solutions for forecasting, revenue recognition, and automation.
  - **Leverage Partnerships**: Build a robust ecosystem of SaaS partners to provide capabilities like HCM, spend management, and subscription billing, allowing Sage Intacct to compete with ERP suites while remaining focused on its core strengths.
  - **Streamline Operations**: Address operational needs like procurement, payroll, and AP automation to offer a more seamless, end-to-end solution for mid-market organizations.

By targeting these five SaaS categories with strategic partnerships, Sage can deliver a complete product experience while maintaining its specialization in **core financials**.

Conversation Highlights

This conversation was loaded with insights, giving us our entire battle landscape on one page. That can take ages to create manually, but this took minutes. It listed our legacy competitors and explained how our general product type solves the problem created by the discontinuities we discovered in the last step. Then, it identified our new-world competitors, listing what types of applications and partnerships we'd need to win.

The following part of this conversation is the cherry on top, crystallizing our edge in the competitive landscape.

The ChatGPT Smart Conversation
PART 2: Finding Competitive Discontinuities

For all the competition's strengths and weaknesses, there is only one area that matters right now: is my competitor better or worse at addressing the *specific screaming pain caused by the discontinuity?*

We know what market shifts are forcing our target customers to act. And we know our top competitor(s) who will also try to capture those hills.

But remember, for all the competition's strengths and weaknesses, there is only one area that matters right now: is my competitor better or worse at addressing the *specific screaming pain caused by the discontinuity?* Who has the most immediate and effective solution to the burning problem when rescuing their kid from the top of the hill? Combining the lessons of Chapters Five and Six, that is what this short Smart Conversation aims to find out.

PROMPT 1

Me: Can you link the ICP pains and discontinuities to the strengths of Sage Intacct and the weaknesses of Oracle Net-Suite?

ChatGPT:
ICP Requirements: Sage Intacct vs. Oracle NetSuite

ICP Requirement	Sage Intacct's Strengths	Oracle NetSuite's Weaknesses
Multi-Entity & Multi-Currency Consolidation	Best-in-class automation for intercompany eliminations & multi-entity consolidation. Real-time global rollups & reporting across 100+ entities.	Rigid intercompany workflows—requires custom scripting for automation. Limited real-time visibility—batch processing slows consolidation.
Automated Financial Reporting & Compliance	Built-in GAAP, IFRS, and tax-ready reporting tailored for family offices. Audit-ready financials with role-based access controls.	Customization-heavy reporting—requires SuiteScript to build dashboards. Slower close process due to NetSuite's batch-based approach.
Investment & Partnership Accounting	Seamless integrations with Addepar, Black Diamond, FundCount. Handles K-1 distributions, carries interest, and fund structures natively.	Investment tracking is not native—requires third-party tools with expensive connectors. Waterfall calculations & capital calls require workarounds.
Audit & Security Controls for Family Trusts	SOC 2 & HIPAA-certified for high-net-worth data security. Role-based permissions secure entity access for heirs & advisors.	Role permissions can be difficult to configure for family offices with layered access needs. Security concerns around complex entity structures.

ICP Requirement	Sage Intacct's Strengths	Oracle NetSuite's Weaknesses
Low IT Overhead & Rapid Deployment	100% cloud-native—no IT maintenance needed. Deploys in weeks, not months.	ERP-like complexity—requires NetSuite Admins & IT teams for management. Higher TCO (Total Cost of Ownership) due to mandatory customizations.

Final Takeaway:

- Family offices cannot afford to delay compliance automation.
- Legacy financial systems are becoming liabilities—high costs, security risks, inefficiencies.
- Next-gen expectations require transparency & governance tools.
- Cloud-based solutions like Sage Intacct future-proof the family office model.

Conversation Highlights

The step produced a focused mini strengths and weaknesses analysis to rapidly justify why Sage Intacct is a better fit to address the ICP's most urgent pains. The study validated that the market is undergoing a shift in which we are naturally strong and our competitor is naturally weak. With this chapter's Smart Conversation, we have the whole market and everything needed to win on a page.

Key Output for Step 4

After this conversation about your competitive landscape amid the market shift, you should have:

- A list of ways your product addresses the true discontinuities of your target market
- A list and in-depth comparison of your top competitors
- A list of key metrics the competition is based on
- A side-by-side assessment of your strengths and your competitor's weaknesses in addressing the customer's discontinuities
- Further clarity on whether to:
  - Pursue: Legacy competitors will be ousted by the market shift; you are stronger than your competitor in fixing the ICP's most urgent and critical pain.
  - Ponder: You and your competitor have similar solutions to fixing the urgent pain; work to see if you can meaningfully differentiate yourself.
  - Pivot: Even if there is a true discontinuity, another new-world competitor has dominated the market first.

CHAPTER 7
All-In-One Positioning Strategy

What incredible insights we have already gotten from these first four steps. Hopefully, by this point, you've got your sights set on the perfect cluster of hills undergoing a major shift, and *you* are just the person to help them. Not only that, but you're armed with specific ways your competition lacks in their area of need. With a growing mastery of Smart Conversations, you are nearly ready to start churning out plans at warp speed.

Many marketing and sales professionals will jump from this point straight into messaging. They want to start putting together the words, tone, and phrasing to finally help the customer see why they *belong* together! It's almost too tempting to resist.

However, to jump into messaging now would be to miss a *critical step*: positioning.

Positioning is the stage in which a company consolidates all it has learned into a distinct, unified identity. This identity, or brand, defines what it offers, who it serves, and how it is unique in relation to others in the market. One's position in the market is generally summarized as a **positioning statement** with two primary functions.

The positioning statement's first function is to summarize all the key findings before this step. It is concretely rooted in specific interviews, articles, and data generated by you and ChatGPT—all in one place. It pulls together all relevant information that proves the customer would be *crazy* not to choose you.

The positioning statement's second function is to be the central hub from which all messaging emanates. This ensures consistent messaging across all platforms and that all claims are traceable and grounded.

121

Woe to those who skip this step. Whenever I used to give courses on positioning, I would present a message on the whiteboard. The message was: "Collaboration without borders." It sounds good, like the kind of thing a clever English major would write. I asked the room what company it was for. Everyone stared back with blank faces. One person guessed, "The Red Cross?" And that was a fair guess! But no. This messaging was written for Intacct and used at a trade show in 2016 before I started at the company.

The messaging "sounded good," but had no apparent connection to Intacct's product or competitive advantages. To their detriment, many companies have the same pitfall. I encourage my fellow marketers to walk the trade show floor, look at each stand's messaging, and imagine what other companies that message could apply to. Many, like "collaboration without borders," could apply to just about any company—or industry, for that matter.

This common mistake is just one of many grave side effects when one's messaging is not grounded in their positioning statement. Messaging becomes fluffy, filled with ambiguous statements and unsubstantiated claims. Luckily, this mistake and many more are highly avoidable with a strong positioning statement.

Crafting a Positioning Statement

I'll tell you up front (if you don't already know): a positioning statement is not meant to be pretty. It is not intended to be witty, humorous, elegant, or anything of the like. Rather, it should be robotic, factual, and formulaic.

This is *not* the message that will be seen by your audience; it is to be used by your team to create a variety of messages across platforms in the future. Its requirement is not to be clever but clear.

Below is a classic positioning statement template from the book *Crossing the Chasm* by Geoffrey Moore.[11] It goes as follows:

For [target customer] who [statement of the need or opportunity], the [product name] is a [product category] that provides [statement of key benefit—that is, compelling reason to buy]. Unlike [primary competitive alternative], our product [statement of primary differentiation].

The following is what a positioning statement like this could look like when filled in. For this example, I am using a company called Mindtrip, which is an AI-powered travel platform. This company shares an investor with Intacct, and while it is a new company, the following positioning statement helps one understand it immediately.

Positioning Statement for Mindtrip.ai:

For modern travelers

Who want to explore and book personalized, multistop journeys effortlessly,

Mindtrip.ai is an AI-native travel experience platform

That combines inspiration, planning, and booking into one intelligent, conversational interface.

Unlike traditional booking sites that rely on static filters and fragmented workflows,

Mindtrip.ai understands your travel style, adapts in real time, and builds your trip with you—from dream to departure.

Since *Crossing the Chasm* came out in 1991, this template has become the de facto way of positioning, particularly in tech companies.

---

[11] https://the.gt/geoffrey-moore-positioning-statement/

This template is an excellent outline for a successful positioning statement. However, after reviewing many positioning statements over the years, I noticed a theme. People generally have no problem adhering to the structure, yet the statements often lack the meat to make them compelling.

Here were the most common errors I saw when people tried to implement the classic positioning statement:

- **For:** Not being explicit about the "who"; not leveraging the names of industry-leading companies or firms they already have as customers or are connected with; not being explicit about the whole buying team with their job titles and roles in the procurement process
- **Who need:** Not focusing on the discontinuity; confusing a trigger event in a single account for a true industry-wide shift
- **That provides:** Using words like "better," "faster," and "cheaper" without specific metrics such as "time reduced," "cost reduced," "risk reduced," or "growth increased"
- **Unlike:** Not articulating the advantages; effectively expressing, "We are the same as them, but smaller and with fewer customers."

In light of these common mistakes, I find that marketing people can generate more substantial statements with a more detailed template like the one below.

The Extended Positioning Statement

To help people create meatier, more compelling positioning statements, my team and I crafted the following extended outline with additional prompts and ideas for how one could pack a punch into this concise statement.

- **For**
  - Include buyer personas for each person in the buying team.
  - Include names of companies or firms that are industry leaders and lend credibility to your strength in the micro-vertical.
- **Who need to**
  - Mention the whole industry discontinuity.
  - Mention the impact of the discontinuity.
  - State the critical need.
- **My Product or Company is the only**
  - State your product or service name and category (this one's hard to mess up).
- **That provides**
  - Include metrics that show how you solve the critical need above in terms of the following:
    - Overall benefit
    - Specific time benefit
    - Specific cost benefit
    - Specific growth benefit
    - Specific risk benefit
    - Specific regulatory benefit
- **Unlike**
  - Old-World Competitor 1 (being phased out by discontinuity)
  - Old-World Competitor 2 (being phased out by discontinuity)
  - New-World Competitor 1, and mention weaknesses like the following:
    - Not focused on this micro-vertical
    - No key customers to lend credibility
    - Lack of micro-vertical understanding
    - Lack of critical product functionality needed for this micro-vertical

Below is what the extended positioning statement would look like if it were filled out, keeping Mindtrip as the example. Note that I created this using ChatGPT with little to no expertise in the travel platform industry.

- **For**
  - **Persona**: Digital-first, experience-hungry travelers—from solo explorers to creative professionals, travel advisors, and remote teams—who are tired of cookie-cutter tools and want travel to feel inspiring again.
  - **Companies or firms:** Early adopters and "head buffalo" firms like Remote Year, Selina, and Atlas Obscura already prove there's a massive shift toward intelligent, multi-experience travel planning—and Mindtrip is building the platform to match.
- **Who need to**
  - **Whole industry discontinuity**: Adapt to a fundamental shift in the way people plan and book travel.
  - **Impact of the discontinuity**: AI has changed expectations for how people interact with digital platforms. Travelers no longer want to search, compare, and click—they want to converse, personalize, and explore with guidance that feels intuitive.
  - **Critical need**: A unified platform that can plan, personalize, and book entire travel experiences—not just transactions—in a way that feels effortless and intelligent.
- **Mindtrip.ai is the only travel platform built for the AI era**
- **That provides**
  - A conversational, AI-native platform that plans multi-stop trips the way people actually think—visually, intuitively, and dynamically.
  - **Time benefit**: Design an entire journey—flights, stays, experiences—in minutes, not hours.

○ **Cost benefit**: Eliminate the need for separate planning tools, apps, and coordination across sites.

○ **Future risk benefit**: Reduce booking mistakes, missed connections, and planning fatigue with a single source of intelligent truth.

○ **Future growth benefit**: Support creators, travel advisors, and emerging platforms with scalable, collaborative trip tools.

○ **Fun benefit**: Planning becomes play again—not a chore. Mindtrip brings joy and discovery back to the journey.

• **Unlike**

○ **Old-World Competitors**: Legacy platforms like Expedia, Booking.com, and Google Flights are optimized for filters, clicks, and bookings—not discovery, personalization, or intelligent guidance. These platforms still treat travel as a transactional task, not a creative journey.

○ **New-World Competitors**: New AI competitors like Roam Around or GuideGeek offer clever demos but lack real personalization, platform depth, or integrated booking capability. Most are lightweight interfaces, not serious end-to-end platforms.

Positioning Summary (One-Liner):

Mindtrip.ai is the travel platform built for the AI era—where conversation replaces search, intelligence replaces filters, and planning feels like dreaming out loud.

This extended positioning statement effectively summarizes everything we have mapped out so far: the market, the discontinuity, the competitive landscape, and your key advantages. It captures "Why Switch?" "Why Now?" and "Why Me?" At this critical juncture, research solidifies into an identity and a concise plan.

Positioning: Manual Versus ChatGPT

An expert can create a comprehensive summary of their Go-To-Market strategy on a single page. However, it is challenging to summarize everything about an industry, from the key buyers to the pains and drivers behind those pains.

A summary like this takes a very skilled and particular type of person. Traditionally, it requires a person who is intellectually curious and eager to learn continually. This person is great at interviewing customers and skilled at forming open-ended questions, but also not afraid to drill down on key conversations. They are comfortable moving out of their area of expertise and interviewing others in fields they know nothing about while maintaining their confidence. This person can then convert this knowledge into a sales playbook that can be easily understood and used to equip sales teams. In my experience, this is a rare person, and the best ones I have found are from product marketing, not an industry background.

In the hands of a rare expert like this, an extended position statement can become the foundation for a compelling narrative for potential customers' ears. However, people without this special combination of skills can produce pages and pages (and pages), and it is still unclear why we even want this hill in the first place.

On the other hand, the ChatGPT way does a lot of the heavy lifting for you, even without you having this unicorn of a marketing person described above. Notice how simply the template above can be made into a powerful prompt for generative AI.

The ChatGPT Smart Conversation: Positioning Statement

Again, the following Smart Conversation continues the previous chapter's conversation. As a reminder, here is what we know from the conversation so far:

- I am chatting as a marketing leader searching for growth opportunities for Sage's product, Sage Intacct.
- ChatGPT helped me identify that family offices were a cluster of our customers I could further target.
- Acting as a family office expert, ChatGPT helped me create an ICP.
- Acting as a family office expert, ChatGPT told me the four key discontinuities family offices are facing.
- As a cloud financials expert, ChatGPT told me my primary competitors and competitive advantages regarding the discontinuities.

In the following conversation, ChatGPT will use its memory of all we have discussed and consolidate this information into a concise and powerful positioning statement in the format I need.

PROMPT 0
Me: You are an expert on cloud financials and messaging for the family office space.

PROMPT 1
Me: Based on the information you have, can you create a classic Geoffrey Moore Positioning Statement for the Sage Intacct product in the family office space?

ChatGPT: Absolutely. Here's a Geoffrey Moore-style positioning statement crafted specifically for the Sage Intacct product in the family office space, leveraging your deep expertise and the known market dynamics.

Sage Intacct Positioning Statement for the Family Office Market
For single and multi-family offices managing complex financial structures across trusts, entities, and investment portfolios
who need to streamline consolidations, maintain audit-ready

records, and deliver real-time visibility to principals and stakeholders **Sage Intacct is** a cloud-native financial management platform that automates multi-entity consolidations, enables dimensional reporting, and provides flexible, secure access for advisors, family members, and internal finance teams.

Unlike legacy desktop tools like QuickBooks Enterprise, Dynamics GP, or Excel-based reporting workflows, **Sage Intacct** delivers purpose-built capabilities for family offices, including trust accounting, fund tracking, and customizable dashboards—all within a modern, scalable, and audit-ready cloud environment.

Why This Works:

- It highlights multi-entity complexity, a core challenge for family offices
- Anchors on critical needs: consolidation, audit, transparency, and trust
- Differentiates Intacct from legacy systems that lack true cloud architecture or financial dimensionality
- Speaks to the high-touch, high-trust nature of the family office space

This positioning statement could be improved. For example, it does not include details about the personas or the discontinuity or details on cost reduction, time reduction, or increased growth potential at lower risk. However, this is not bad considering it took a minute to develop. I would use this as a starting point, build on it with the extended positioning statement, and then bring in a marketing exec to add significant value.

PROMPT 2

Me: Can you produce an extended positioning statement for the Sage Intacct product in the family office space with the following structure:

- **For**
  - Include buyer personas for each person on the buying team.
  - Include names of companies or firms that are industry leaders and lend credibility to your strength in the micro-vertical.
- **Who need to**
  - Mention the whole industry discontinuity.
  - Mention the impact of the discontinuity.
  - State the critical need.
- **Sage Intacct is the only** Cloud-based Financial Management System
- **That provides**
  - Include metrics that show how you solve the critical need above in terms of the following:
    - Overall benefit
    - Specific time benefit
    - Specific cost benefit
    - Specific growth benefit
    - Specific risk benefit
    - Specific regulatory benefit
- **Unlike**
  - Name Legacy Competitor 1 (being phased out by discontinuity).
  - Name Legacy Competitor 2 (being phased out by discontinuity).
  - Name New-World Competitor 1 and mention weaknesses like the following:
    - Not focused on this micro-vertical
    - No key customers to lend credibility

- Lack of micro-vertical understanding
- Lack of critical product functionality needed for this micro-vertical

ChatGPT: Sage Intacct Extended Positioning Statement for Family Offices
Based on the structure provided and the information from the interviews, here's an extended positioning statement for the Sage Intacct product.

- **For:**
    - **Personas:** CFOs, Controllers, and financial executives in single and multi-family offices who manage complex financial structures across multiple entities, trusts, and investment vehicles—and are responsible for ensuring transparency, control, and reporting accuracy to high-net-worth families and boards.
    - **Companies/Firms:** And for firms like Halstatt and DFO—the "head buffalos" leading the modernization of the family office model—who have shown the need for secure, scalable, real-time financial infrastructure that supports the demands of today's ultra-complex wealth management structures.
- **Who need to:**
    - **Adapt to a major discontinuity in the family office space:** The traditional model of siloed systems, spreadsheets, and manual consolidations is breaking down under the pressure of multi-entity complexity, intergenerational transparency, and real-time reporting expectations from principals and beneficiaries.
    - **Impact of the Discontinuity:** Family offices are under increasing pressure to:
        - Produce audit-ready, fund-specific reporting on demand

- Support intergenerational financial visibility
- Meet more complex regulatory compliance and governance expectations
- Scale without scaling staff, especially in a multi-family or outsourced finance model

- **Sage Intacct is the only:** cloud financials product
- **That provides:** a purpose-built cloud financial management platform that enables family offices to automate consolidations across hundreds of trusts, LLCs, and partnerships.

  o **Critical need**: A modern, cloud-native financial system that can centralize financial operations, automate multi-entity consolidations, and deliver dimensional reporting that reflects the real structure of family wealth—all with the audit trail, security, and customization that ultra high-net-worth families demand.

  o **Time benefit**: Reduce month-end close from weeks to days by eliminating manual consolidations and Excel workarounds.

  o **Cost benefit**: Avoid the headcount and IT infrastructure typically required to manage entity sprawl.

  o **Growth benefit**: Enable the finance team to support new family entities, philanthropic arms, or investment vehicles without retooling the system.

  o **Risk benefit**: Improve audit outcomes, reduce operational risk, and ensure data integrity across complex ownership structures.

  o **Regulatory benefit**: Stay ahead of increasingly complex compliance frameworks with built-in fund tracking, audit logs, and GAAP/FASB reporting alignment.

- **Unlike:**
  - **Old-World Competitors:** Legacy on-premises systems (e.g., QuickBooks Enterprise, Microsoft Dynamics GP, or proprietary family office stacks) are brittle, spreadsheet-reliant, and unable to scale or support secure, real-time reporting without major IT overhead.
  - **New-World Competitors:** Generic cloud accounting systems (e.g., NetSuite, Xero, QuickBooks Online), which lack deep multi-entity, dimensional fund tracking, and family-office-level control—and were built for startups, not stewardship.

Summary Line:
Sage Intacct is the only cloud-native financial platform designed to meet the complexity, control, and transparency required by modern family offices—built to scale wealth stewardship into the next generation.

Conversation Highlights

This extended positioning statement leverages insights on Sage Intacct's unique value propositions and differentiators. It effectively consolidates all we have learned so far and explains why the Sage Intacct product is the obvious choice against both legacy competitors and other new-world competition. *And* it manages to do so in less than three hundred words, which is quite impressive.

This is an internal document that provides the foundation for how we present ourselves to the world, attack the hills, and measure success in a data-driven way. A marketing executive can now build upon this and infuse it with even more concrete metrics.

Key Output for Step 5

After this step, you have the following for your micro-vertical:

- The one-page extended positioning statement summarizing the strategy and Go-To-Market for the micro-vertical
- A starting point to adapt if you want to target other related micro-verticals next

There is no "pursue, pause, or pivot" here since this step consolidates all we have done; no new information has been added. But even at this stage, don't be afraid to qualify out a micro-vertical if you discover red flags you didn't see before.

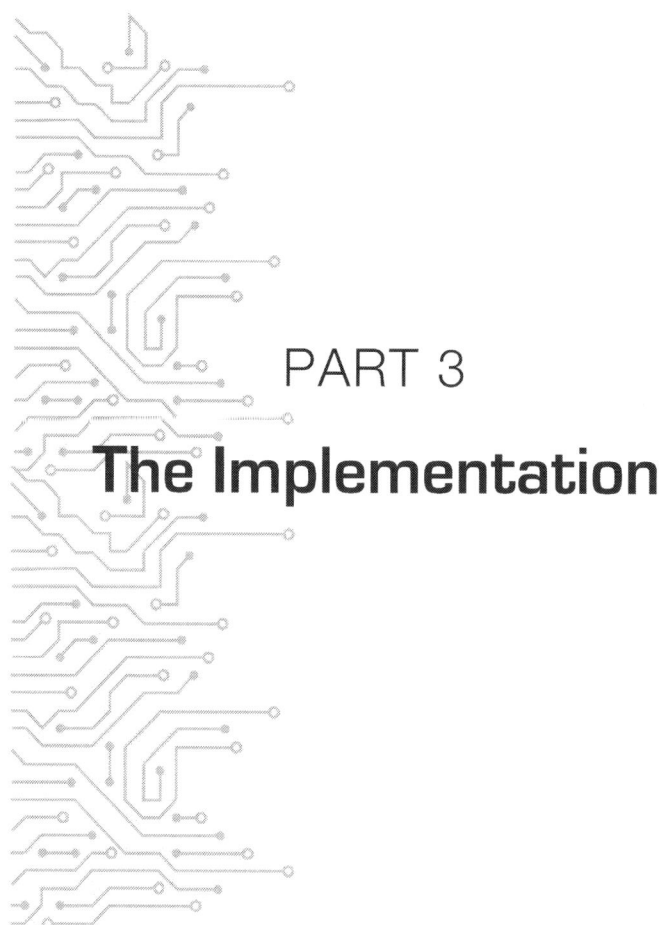

PART 3

The Implementation

CHAPTER 8
Power Messaging the ChatGPT Way

Everything we have done so far has been internal preparation: Choosing a hill to target, studying the population, spotting mass movements, surveying the competition, and plotting our position. While this may seem like a lot of preparation, these steps are akin to the deep root system beneath a tree. These preparations make way for a robust and sustainable outward sprout. It will surely outlast the nearby trees that eagerly sprang up from the ground with no anchoring strategy beneath the surface.

While this chapter is still an extension of that preparation, it marks a shift outward towards implementation. Here, we focus on how we will communicate with the residents of the hills we want to win over.

This chapter is about **messaging**: how a company communicates the value of its product to its target audience. Messaging includes words, tone, and phrasing. It focuses on the product's value and is tailored to each specific audience. It also gives the customer a sense of the company's overall identity and personality.

Unfortunately, many companies come across as a bit "socially awkward" upon their first real interaction with a customer. This can be for many reasons. As we've discussed, messaging can come across as tone-deaf because it does not speak directly about the market shift.

Another pitfall is that, in trying to appeal to many audiences at once, many companies produce broad, bland, and nonspecific messaging. It's like if someone said, "We sell supplies for sports with round, inflated balls!" People don't talk that way. People say, "I love basketball. I love the Warriors. Steph Curry is my favorite player." Knowing this, a marketer might instead say, "We sell basketball supplies, including the knee pads used by Steph Curry."

If you listen to how customers talk, you can even harness the language *they* use in your messaging. Then, you may not need to say "basketball supplies" at all—instead, you can say "Ball is life," and they will know what you sell. There is so much opportunity here, yet much messaging falls into the "round inflated balls" category.

Yet another fumble is failing to communicate the difference between you and the competition. I once reviewed a plan in which the messaging was good on the surface, but it lacked any focus on why we were a better choice than the competition (see the "unlike" section in the chapter on positioning). It effectively stated, "We are the same as the competition but smaller and with fewer customers." It wasn't exactly putting our best foot forward.

As you can see, even with a great market, messaging can be misguided in many ways.

Crafting Differentiated Power Messaging

The good news is that these messaging pitfalls are highly avoidable through **Differentiated Power Messaging**. Differentiated Power Messaging is a messaging paradigm I created to highlight the value proposition, the competitive advantage, and authority in the market. Differentiated Power Messaging meets the following six basic principles. It is:

1. **Compelling:** It focuses on the customer's urgent need.
2. **Fact-driven:** It uses industry-relevant metrics and real customer stories to demonstrate value.
3. **Differentiated:** It identifies your competitive advantage(s).
4. **Defensible:** The advantage cannot be easily copied or outdone by the competition.

5. **Customer-focused:** It centers customer stories to describe both what the company does and what the product does.

6. **Intuitively believable:** No explanation is required by a human; it just makes sense.

Most importantly, if you have gone through the process, Differentiated Power Messaging is not so difficult. It is a classic Karate Kid "wax on, wax off" moment. This is because, if you have taken the time to create a solid positioning statement, you already have the majority of what you will need to create incredibly effective power messaging. Recall what you filled out for the classic Geoffrey Moore positioning statement:

> For [target customer] who [statement of the need or opportunity], the [product name] is a [product category] that provides [statement of key benefit—that is, compelling reason to buy]. Unlike [primary competitive alternative], our product [statement of primary differentiation].

In the extended positioning statement, you provided even more detailed information about your target market, discontinuity, value statement, competitive edge, and more. You've already gathered and articulated the material to satisfy all six power messaging principles.

By basing your messaging on the positioning statement, you also ensure your claims are not fluffy and groundless promises. Your positioning statement came from real data, interviews, case studies, and research in prior stages. If your messaging is rooted in this, you'll have a defense for anyone who might challenge you.

The most common mistake I have seen is people using their positioning statement as their messaging. To be clear, this is *not* what I am advocating for. The positioning statement is a summary—it is ugly and robotic. It is not to be used externally, but it makes a perfect foundation from which to craft many different types of effective messages.

Differentiated Power Messaging Structures That Work

So, how do you turn your positioning statement into Differentiated Power Messaging? You do so by learning to adapt your positioning material into new formats that fit the customer and the context. There are multiple messaging structures, but here, I will present the four I have found to be most effective.

Power Messaging Structure #1: The High-Value Pitch

One of the more well-known messaging formats is the elevator pitch. When I worked at Documentum, the team developed a particular elevator pitch format that was eventually used as a case study in Harvard Business School's MBA course as a testament to its usefulness.[12]

Here's an example of the pitch, adapted to pharmaceutical companies:

> Documentum works with leading pharmaceutical companies such as Pfizer, Glaxo, and Merck to reduce the time it takes to process a global New Drug Application from 18 months to 6 weeks, allowing them to generate an additional one million dollars per day.

Here is another example of the pitch format for our work in swaps and derivatives processing on Wall Street:

> Documentum works with leading Wall Street firms such as Lehman, Morgan, and Merrill to take feeds directly from Cats and Infinity and reduce the time to process plain vanillas, exotics, and baskets from days to T+0, reducing risk exposure by billions of dollars daily. The

---

[12] Further examples developed at Documentum and used in Harvard's MBA course can be found at this website: https://www.hbs.edu/faculty/Pages/item.aspx?num=28459.

leading law firm, Linklaters, even provides ISDA agreements directly in the product.

- **Pitch template:**
  [Company name] works with leading [industry name] companies such as [company names] to enable them to [value proposition based on time, cost, growth and/or risk], allowing them to [highlight key benefit].

- **Strengths:**
  This is effectively the "show me the money" pitch, as it rapidly highlights the benefit statement regarding the most critical metrics: cost, time, growth, and risk. By starting with industry-leading companies you're already connected with, you establish your credibility up front. The pitch uses insider language to establish deep understanding, and it communicates quickly: "We work with firms like yours every day of the week. You'd be crazy to choose anyone else."

- **Best uses:**
  This pitch type is ideal when introducing yourself to a stranger—in the elevator, at a networking event, or at a trade show stand, for example. The stranger might be a prospective customer, a potential partner, or a future investor. The pitch can be used by large companies with a sturdy customer base or by newer companies that have managed to win over a key member of the listener's network.

Power Messaging Structure #2: The Cage Match Pitch

The Cage Match Pitch structure was inspired by the "Droid Does" campaign, which seemed to be nearly everywhere one looked in 2009. This campaign was Verizon and Motorola's hundred-million-dollar marketing push to promote the first line of Android smartphones, particularly the Motorola Droid. The aggressive yet memorable campaign highlighted the features or abilities the Droid phone could do that the iPhone could not. Their tagline was "iDon't," capitalizing on specific limitations of its biggest competitor.

Here is an example of the messaging from a commercial released on November 6th, 2009:

> "iDon't have a real keyboard.
> iDon't run simultaneous apps.
> iDon't take 5 megapixel pictures.
> iDon't customize.
> iDon't run widgets.
> iDon't allow open development.
> iDon't take pictures in the dark.
> iDon't have interchangeable batteries.
> Everything iDon't, Droid Does."[13]

Besides its focus on feature limitations, the other notable part of this campaign is that it focused on a single competitor. Just like in a cage match, two go into the ring, but only one comes out victorious.[14] The fight is focused on the other top competitor, and only one company comes out on top as the market leader.

Ultimately, Android didn't exactly turn out to be the "iPhone killer" Verizon was betting on. Yet the campaign's effect shouldn't be dismissed simply because the iPhone lives on. In 2009, there were many contenders for who would lead in smartphones, including Symbian, BlackBerry, Windows Mobile, and the lingering Palm OS of PalmPilot fame. Android successfully established itself as *the* alternative to the iPhone. Of course, its success involved many factors (the support of Google certainly helped). But even so, it's undeniable that the Droid Does

---

[13] https://www.youtube.com/watch?v=e52TSXwj774

[14] This strategy was also described in John Zagula and Richard Tong's 2004 book, *The Marketing Playbook*. They describe this approach as a "drag race," paralleling the two-player race in which the fastest car wins.

campaign played a huge role in its achievements. Android continues to grow its cult following of users who swear by superior functionality. The Droid Does campaign lives on in spirit.[15]

Working for Sage, my team created our own "Droid Does" campaign against our primary competitor. We used this in every presentation, tradeshow, etc.:

The healthcare-focused Droid Does campaign is as follows:
"Is your cloud financial system:
Able to consolidate 10's of legal entities in
seconds across multiple practices?
HIPAA compliant with a Business Associate
Agreement (BAA)?
Chosen by the AICPA and IFAC?[16]
Intacct is. Find out more here."

Sage was successful against its primary competitor, in large part due to the strength of the above messaging, which was used across multiple channels.

Here are three additional examples I created using ChatGPT for the AI-driven travel company, Mindtrip:

Does your travel platform plan an entire multi-destination journey in minutes—with AI that actually understands your style?
Does it combine booking, itineraries, inspiration, and recommendations—all in one intuitive experience?
Does it let you chat with your trip—not just click and search?
Mindtrip.ai does.

---

[15] https://www.theverge.com/2018/10/24/18017988/android-verizon-motorola-droid-history

[16] These are two important organizations in accounting: the American Institute of Certified Public Accountants (AICPA) and the International Federation of Accountants (IFAC).

Does your trip planner think beyond flights and hotels—and suggest hidden gems you didn't even know you wanted?
Does it understand your preferences and budget—and adapt your itinerary on the fly?
Does it feel more like a conversation with a savvy travel agent than a form to fill out?
Mindtrip.ai does.

Does your platform let you design complex, multi-country trips—without 37 browser tabs?
Does it optimize for time, cost, and experience—not just cheapest flights?
Does it give you a travel assistant, not just a search box?
Mindtrip.ai does.

Each clearly demonstrates Mindtrip's competitive advantage. The first could be used in a match against other travel platforms, the second could be used against other trip planners, and the third could be used against more general platforms. Each of these is rooted in the positioning statement with strong and concrete differentiation: it is not just another trip planner; it is the future of travel in the AI era.

- **Pitch template:**
  Choose one competitor and compare your product with theirs, function by function, highlighting their shortcomings compared to yours.
  Does your [category] do [leading differentiator A]?
  Does your [category] do [leading differentiator B]?
  Does your [category] do [leading differentiator C]?
  [Our company/product] does.

- **Strengths:**
  This messaging structure is simple, direct, and extremely easy for a customer to grasp. It highlights your benefit and value statement. And by focusing on one competitor, you can get very specific with a feature-by-feature breakdown. You have the opportunity to pinpoint all those small yet incredibly annoying or painstaking parts of the opposite product that drive their customers up the wall. It's a compelling way to win converts, especially if you can tie your strengths and their weaknesses to the problem caused by the discontinuity. This is what we did in the above Sage example, where the problem created by the discontinuity was the need to consolidate hundreds of legal entities—or in the case of healthcare, be HIPAA compliant.

- **Best uses:**
  This messaging can be used on your website, ads, commercials, social media, and at trade shows.

Power Messaging Structure #3: The Metaphor Pitch
Marc Benioff is a legend in the industry and a pioneer of cloud computing and SaaS. In an interview with Forbes (and in his book *Behind the Cloud*), he showed how much thought he put into telling the Salesforce story. He had to. People were deeply ingrained in a legacy system called Siebel, and he was trying to bring them into the future. Yet he was trying to sell people on something that they had absolutely no grid for yet.

In the interview, he said, "I spend a lot of time creating metaphors to explain what we do. For example, early on, I explained what we did with the metaphor, 'Salesforce.com is Amazon.com meets Siebel Systems.' Later, when we launched AppExchange, we called it 'the eBay of enterprise software.' You have to be able to relate your product to something familiar."[17]

Bennioff's metaphor paid off. By relating it to the existing Siebel System, he communicated to users that his system would still allow them to perform all the basic functions they were used to and relied on. And by comparing it to Amazon, he also associated his product with someone new but that people enjoyed and understood. Amazon was new and easy to use with clearly organized tabs for (in those days) books and CDs. In short, he communicated that Salesforce had the core functionality of Siebel with the futurism and simplicity of Amazon.

- **Pitch template:**
  My [new product] is [new beloved product] meets [old familiar product or category].

- **Strengths:**
  This framework is concise and intuitive, saying multitudes with very little.

  For this to work, you must choose a metaphor outside your own category, or the comparison may cause confusion and create trademark issues. You also must select other companies that your reader is familiar with.

  When these requirements are met, this form of Differentiated Power Messaging gives your prospect a grid for something they haven't heard of before and, like Benioff says, frames it through the lens of the familiar and loved. It says, "You won't lose what you love from the old system. But you'll also gain all these things you love with a new system." The customer wins all around.

---

[17] [17]https://www.forbes.com/sites/carminegallo/2020/08/26/the-communication-skills-marc-benioff-says-they-dont-teach-you-in-business-school/?sh=2216ee923294

- **Best uses:**
  This messaging structure is especially effective when you introduce a type of product customers are not totally familiar with, like a whole new product category. It can also be used to gain buy-in from your employees and investors. It is excellent for your website, ads, trade shows, etc.

Power Messaging Structure #4: The Best-of-Both Pitch

The final messaging structure here is the "Best-of-Both." It is similar to the Marc Benioff metaphor in that it relates two known products to explain your unknown product. However, in the Marc Benioff example, the two known products are 1) the legacy product and 2) a new-world product. In this structure, you are not necessarily invoking "new-world versus old-world." Instead, you would use the comparison to highlight benefits like saving time, cost, risk, or convenience.[18]

One example is when I worked at a company called Alfresco. In its day, it was the most valuable private open-source company in the world and the open-source leader for content management. But when I joined, it was a relatively small business with twelve employees and some big goals.

In Alfresco's battle landscape, we had the high-end/enterprise players: Documentum, FileNet, and OpenText. These million-dollar products needed an extremely high-value application to justify the price tag and the cost of a major Systems Integrator to roll it out. On the low end: the much-used but slow and intensely disliked shared file drive.

Here, there were high-end luxury enterprise products that were too expensive for the masses, and then there was a low-end cheap product that was a pain to use. As a small business, we didn't have anywhere near the resources or workforce to make war with the giants. However, between the low-end and high-end was

---

[18] The "Best-of-Both" structure was first presented in Zagula and Tong's book, *The Marketing Playbook*.

149

a massive market potential for Alfresco (as well as emerging products like SharePoint from Microsoft and later Dropbox and Box).
The Alfresco messaging was:

"The Open-Source alternative to ECM."
(Enterprise Content Management)

The subliminal message was, "The Open-Source alternative to Documentum at a tenth of the cost." This pitch was aided by the fact that Documentum co-founder John Newton was also the co-founder of Alfresco. Prospects could trust they would get a luxury quality at a much more reasonable price tag.

Comparisons can revolve around price, like the one above, like saying, "Our hotel provides the luxury of an Intercontinental hotel with the price of a Marriott Courtyard," or "Our car is like getting a Mercedes for the price of a Toyota." However, they can also revolve around other factors. For example, one could say, "Canva combines the sophistication of the Adobe Creative Cloud with the simplicity of a tool that anyone in marketing can use."

- **Pitch template:**
  [My product] provides the [strength] of [product A] combined with the [strength] of [product 2]. The phrasing can, of course, be adapted as you like, but this is the gist.

- **Strengths:**
  This product-centered pitch is intuitive and, like the prior metaphors, communicates a great deal with very little. It plays on established brands' known strengths and weaknesses to position yourself as the "best-of-both-worlds" option.

- **Best uses:**
  This structure is an excellent answer to the question, "How does your product compare to [another product on the market]?" It works especially well if you are providing

an alternative to known systems that are still unsatisfying or inaccessible to a large market of users. Use this for elevator pitches, your website, ad campaigns, and tradeshows.

Turbocharge Your Message Checklists

Of course, messaging is a broad term, and you may need more forms of messaging, like a tagline, for example. Any structure you need, you can plug into ChatGPT for ideas. But before we move on to how ChatGPT can help you create messages in these structures, I want to emphasize that there is an essential human element here. ChatGPT is an excellent collaborator, but there is always a need for a human to check these messaging ideas, not taking them at face value, but testing them against the checklist of messaging best practices.

Use the following checklists as a guideline as you evaluate ideas from AI and your team.

Always:

- Base your messaging on the positioning statement. (This keeps it fact-based, customer-focused, and differentiated.)
- Make your messaging as personal as possible (at the micro-vertical level).
- Think of the ten-second rule. (Is the message immediately clear and compelling without someone explaining it?)
- Focus your message on the discontinuity experienced by the whole industry.
- Use tangible metrics and stories of overcoming the pain brought on by the discontinuity (not generalized "better, faster, cheaper, easier" statements).
- Maintain consistency across multiple channels (as the prospect will likely engage with you through numerous avenues even before your first conversation).

151

- Check the responsiveness of your design. (Check mobile view and how easy it is to enter forms when people respond to your messaging.)

Never:
- Leave the meat until the end. (Start with the punchline.)
- Replace great messaging because you're bored with it. (This sin is done by some of the best, most intelligent marketing people I know.)
- Be a baby dinosaur. (Don't copy the strategy or messaging of the legacy giant, no matter how good it is; you can't beat them at their own game just by being smaller.)
- Make messaging decisions on opinions alone. (Utilize data from web properties, landing pages, ads, subject lines, social posts, trade show stands, A/B testing, etc.)

Lastly, think about your message in expanding tiers. The first, most condensed message gets someone to say, "Tell me more." Once you have their attention, you expand to the next tier, in which you can bring in more metrics, specifics, and customer stories.

Power Messaging: Manual Versus ChatGPT

Developing great power messaging takes a long time and is a rare skill. But what makes the process even more difficult is that *everybody* has an opinion. Who can argue with the option the CEO's wife likes best?

Messaging by committee is always a challenge, but it is almost impossible to do it consistently at scale. Often, companies outsource messaging, as it is impossible to achieve internal consensus.

However, the above messaging structures (and having the positioning statement) make it incredibly easy to generate ideas en masse through AI collaboration. Imagine a world where it is easy to create high-quality messaging. You can generate tens of messages as easily as one. That's pretty incredible!

And what's more: You can ask for feedback from not a single subjective person but a whole advisory board of your best customers, available 24/7. You can pit your best messages against each other and ask ChatGPT to create a competition, starting with eight messages, choosing the top four, then the top two, then the top one—with explanations for every choice, which you, the human, can evaluate and make decisions upon.

This is the next generation, AI-first way of Differentiated Power Messaging. This way builds on traditional messaging wisdom, decreases subjectivity and confusion, and produces many precise options with speed and explicit rationale.

The ChatGPT Smart Conversation: Differentiated Power Messaging

Generative messaging uses the full power of Gen AI from the elevator pitch to the tagline. The following Smart Conversation continues from the last.

- I am chatting as a marketing leader searching for growth opportunities for Sage's product, Sage Intacct.
- ChatGPT helped me identify that family offices were a cluster of our customers I could further target.
- As a family office expert, ChatGPT helped me create an ICP, identify discontinuities, and understand the competitive landscape.
- Lastly, ChatGPT helped summarize my strengths and competitive advantages in a positioning statement.

The following conversation will demonstrate a few of the countless messaging structures that ChatGPT can help customize.

The High-Value Pitch Structure

PROMPT 1

Me: Based on the positioning statement, can you create a 50-word elevator pitch demonstrating understanding of the customer, discontinuity, and competitive advantages?

ChatGPT: Sage Intacct is the financial backbone for high-growth, data-driven CFOs and CIOs managing over a trillion dollars in AUM. We provide real-time, continuous multi-entity consolidation, reducing time and costs while ensuring full GAAP compliance. Unlike competitors, Sage deeply understands and supports the unique needs of family offices through a dedicated community.

PROMPT 2

Me: Can you create a 25-word messaging statement encompassing the single most powerful differentiator?

ChatGPT: Sage Intacct provides real-time, continuous multi-entity consolidation, drastically reducing time and costs, uniquely tailored for family offices with a deep understanding of their specific needs.

PROMPT 3

Me: Can you create a 10-word messaging statement encompassing the single most powerful differentiator?

ChatGPT: Sage Intacct delivers real-time, continuous multi-entity consolidation for family offices.

PROMPT 4

Me: Can you create a tagline encompassing the single most powerful differentiator?

ChatGPT: "Real-Time Multi-Entity Consolidation for Family Offices"

The Cage Match Structure

PROMPT 5

Me: Based on the extended positioning statement, can you develop messaging using the "Droid Does" campaign structure of:

- Does your [category] do [leading differentiator A]?
- Does your [category] do [leading differentiator B]?
- Does your [category] do [leading differentiator C]?
- Sage Intacct Does.

ChatGPT: Certainly! Here's the messaging using the Cage Match campaign structure:

- Does your financial solution do real-time, continuous, multi-entity consolidation?
- Does your financial solution reduce consolidation time from 100 hours to minutes?
- Does your financial solution save $2 million in family office costs?
- Sage Intacct Does.

The Metaphor Structure

PROMPT 6

Me: Based on the extended positioning statement, can you develop messaging using the Metaphor messaging structure Marc Benioff used to describe Salesforce: "Salesforce.com is Amazon.com meets Siebel Systems."

ChatGPT: Sage Intacct is the financial Canva for your family office.

This metaphor conveys that Sage Intacct empowers you to design and customize your financial workflows with the same simplicity that Canva brings to design.

The Best-of-Both Structure

PROMPT 7
Me: Based on the extended positioning statement, can you develop messaging using the Best-of-Both campaign structure: "[My product] provides the [strength] of [product A] combined with the [strength] of [product 2]?"

ChatGPT: Sage Intacct provides the intelligence of AI-powered automation combined with the trusted accuracy of GAAP-compliant accounting.

This highlights automation while reinforcing compliance for CFOs and controllers.

Finding the Winning Message

For *any* messaging structure (a slogan, Impact Pitch, etc.), you can ask ChatGPT for multiple options—say eight, for example. Then you can ask it to run a competition between the options to see which is best. It also tells you *why* that one is best and why each of the others was eliminated. It is an excellent brainstorming tool with objective rationale to consider. You can use the winners in the next chapter's campaign. Here is an example of one such competition.

Running a Competition

PROMPT 8

Me: You are a messaging expert in cloud accounting and family office spaces. Based on the Metaphor messaging structure, can you create eight variations for Sage Intacct?

ChatGPT:

1. **"Sage Intacct is the financial Canva of your business."**
   Empowering you to design and customize your financial workflows with the same simplicity and creativity that Canva brings to design.

2. **"Sage Intacct is the Netflix of financial management."**
   Offering a personalized, on-demand experience for your business finances, Intacct adapts to your needs, just like Netflix curates your favorite shows.

3. **"Sage Intacct is the Uber of accounting."**
   Revolutionizing financial management by simplifying complex processes and delivering fast, reliable insights whenever and wherever you need them.

4. **"Sage Intacct is the Shopify of financial systems."**
   Enabling you to scale and manage your financial operations with the same agility and ease that Shopify brings to online businesses.

5. **"Sage Intacct is the Airbnb of finance."**
   Creating a connected, flexible platform that brings your financial data together, just as Airbnb connects people with unique places to stay.

6. **"Sage Intacct is the Salesforce of accounting."**
   Built to empower your financial team the way Salesforce empowers sales—streamlining workflows and delivering actionable insights at scale.

7. **"Sage Intacct is the Zoom of financial collaboration."**
   Making financial management as seamless and collaborative as Zoom makes communication—simple, intuitive, and always accessible.

8. **"Sage Intacct is the Slack of financial systems."**
   Enabling real-time collaboration and communication across your financial team, Intacct works as intuitively as Slack does for messaging.

PROMPT 9
Me: Can you create a competition to see which has the best messaging and show me the top four, two, and one?

ChatGPT:
Top 4
- "Sage Intacct is the financial Canva of your business."
- "Sage Intacct is the Uber of accounting."
- "Sage Intacct is the Airbnb of finance."
- "Sage Intacct is the Zoom of financial collaboration."

Top 2
- "Sage Intacct is the financial Canva of your business."
- "Sage Intacct is the Zoom of financial collaboration."

Winner
- "Sage Intacct is the Zoom of financial collaboration."

158

The winner and top two were selected based on a simulated decision process that can be refined with real-world input. Here's the rationale for the selection:

- Relatability: Zoom is widely recognized as a game-changing tool for remote communication. Its metaphor aligns with the idea of simplifying collaboration in complex environments.
- Clarity: The metaphor immediately communicates the idea of real-time, accessible, and intuitive collaboration, which is a key benefit for financial management software.
- Modern Appeal: It ties Intacct to a leading SaaS platform known for enabling digital transformation, making it highly relevant and aspirational for tech-savvy audiences.

Top 2:
- **"Sage Intacct is the Zoom of financial collaboration."**
  - This entry carried the same strengths that made it the winner.
- **"Sage Intacct is the financial Canva of your business."**
  - Creativity: Canva is associated with empowering non-designers to achieve professional results effortlessly, making this metaphor resonate with financial teams seeking user-friendly tools.
  - Customizability: The messaging conveys that Intacct allows businesses to tailor their financial workflows, similar to how Canva enables creative expression.

Why Others Didn't Make the Cut:

- **"Sage Intacct is the Uber of accounting."**
  - o The metaphor implies disruption, but the association with transportation might not resonate with financial teams.
- **"Sage Intacct is the Airbnb of finance."**
  - o Innovative, but might not connect clearly with financial collaboration or operational excellence.

It is extraordinary that ChatGPT can run a competition like this and tell you the top choice. But of course, the top choice may depend on who you are presenting to. ChatGPT lets us tailor to an even more individual level.

ChatGPT can mimic you presenting these options to a key decision maker to identify their top choice. At this step, choose a decision maker at an influential company in your cluster. Load their public profile and other information, and ask ChatGPT for that person's reaction to your messaging and position.

This is the new-world of the ChatGPT ultra native that is not just an automation of the old way but a way to smoke the old way.

For the following example, let's say I am the decision maker.

UPLOAD:

Ian Howells' public LinkedIn profile PDF, recent interviews, blog posts, quotes from the annual report, etc.

PROMPT 10

Me: What messaging would Ian Howells prefer and why?

ChatGPT: Given Ian Howells' extensive expertise in marketing and his history with Sage, he would likely favor messaging that aligns with his strategic focus on micro-vertical marketing and clear, customer-centric storytelling.

Preferred messaging based on his leadership style and priorities:

- **"Sage Intacct is the Zoom of financial collaboration."**
  - Why Ian might prefer it: Ian has a strong focus on empowering teams and delivering clear, transformative value to customers. This messaging emphasizes simplicity, accessibility, and real-time collaboration — core needs for financial teams.
- **"Sage Intacct is the financial Canva of your business."**
  - Why Ian might prefer it: Canva's metaphor resonates with empowerment and customization, which aligns with Ian's micro-vertical approach of tailoring solutions to specific industries.

Why These Two:

- **Strategic Fit:** Both messages directly tie to enabling businesses through modern, intuitive platforms, reflecting Ian's AI-driven marketing strategies.
- **Clarity and Emotional Appeal:** They present Sage Intacct as approachable yet transformative, striking a balance between relatability and innovation—key elements in Ian's past messaging success.

Would you like a detailed refinement of these options for a campaign or specific audience?

Conversation Highlights

The world in which you can easily create, tailor, and test a dozen messages in minutes is here now. With the templates and Smart Conversation shown in this chapter, you are now equipped with a Messaging Playbook that can be used with any campaign. This playbook eliminates the need for a "fire drill" to come up with ideas and gain consensus whenever a new message is needed.

The Messaging Playbook is a living document that mirrors our dynamic landscape. Whenever a request that has not already been created comes up, add it to the playbook. If a message stops working, flag it. Research why and consider removing it from the playbook. If a competitor has worked out how to beat a particular message, research and adjust the course again. You can adapt this to any number of shifting micro-verticals, market shifts, and competitive landscapes.

It is especially incredible that ChatGPT can use publicly available information to predict which messaging will be most effective with a single person. Imagine the ground you can cover at this rate, tailoring messages even to an individual at a company in seconds. This is power messaging like never before.

Key Output for Step 6

For each micro-vertical you decide to pursue, you now have your ammunition—a Messaging Playbook complete with the following:

- A variety of concise, compelling messages, based on the facts from the positioning statement, for contexts like the elevator pitch, website copy, PPC, ads, trade shows, and 1:1 conversations
- A way to rapidly test which messages are best
- A way to rapidly tailor these messages to any individual or context

CHAPTER 9
The "Wall of Sound" Campaign

You've got your target. You understand them. You know the shift they're experiencing, and you've got the solution that the competition does not. You've mapped out your position and loaded up entire sequences of precise power messaging. Finally, there's nothing left to do but go in for the charge.

This is where the rubber meets the road. It's time to get your messaging out to your target audience. But how?

Many companies will spend millions and millions of dollars on a marketing campaign that yields sparse results. The leads it delivers are laborious to convert. The pipeline is broken and leaky. The dollars do not go far enough.

The steps we have already taken greatly help prevent this situation. However, it is still possible to encounter this if we have excellent weapons in our arsenal but no idea where or how to aim them.

Let me give you a real-world example of what this looks like when done effectively. In 2016, when Intacct first pursued the family office micro-vertical, we did all the previous steps manually. Once it was time to send out our messaging and attack the hill, we knew exactly where to aim. That year, we passed on some of the biggest general business trade shows for the first time in our company's history. That move was controversial. After all, weren't we missing out on a huge population? The population was huge, but it was also hugely general.

Instead, we focused our efforts and budget on our much smaller micro-vertical. Through research and interviews, we learned all the insider information channels, meetings, magazines, associations, etc. that the family office space relied on. We bombarded each of those with our best messages, bombarded their digital world, and showed up at all their in-person events.

A conversation I had with one of our customers illustrates the effectiveness of our strategy well. At that time, Sage had volunteered to sponsor a charity event for an organization dedicated to parents of children with serious illnesses. It was a good thing to do all around: We wanted to support the organization; companies we partnered with were present; a CFO in our micro-vertical was on the board of the charity. It wasn't anything flashy. It was a rather niche event that most others in the larger business world would not have known about or cared to spend their time on.

However, that was just what we wanted. We didn't want it to feel like we only contacted people when trying to sell something; we wanted to be genuinely ingrained in their community.

I was standing at a table, mingling with a drink in hand, when our customer, the CFO, turned the corner. I watched him do a double-take as we made eye contact. I gave him a wave, and he suddenly burst into laughter.

He walked over to me, shaking his head as he bellowed, "*You're* here? *Of course* you're here! You guys are everywhere I look!"

He arrived beside me and slapped me on the back. "Every time I search online, every association meeting, every analyst conversation. It's always you guys. And none of your competition is there. I don't know how you do it, but I feel like I'm surrounded by a wall of sound saying your company's name over and over again."

"A wall of sound? I like that." I chuckled back at him. "Cheers."

The term "wall of sound" is a musical technique often used in orchestras. It uses a layered arrangement of instruments to create a sound—more of an experience—that is dense, rich, and immersive. That is what our messaging felt like to him. He felt like we surrounded him. We did not have to convince him of anything. With how we positioned our messages, we were framed as the obvious and only real choice.

What the man said was true. We had created what I now call a **Wall of Sound Campaign**: a marketing campaign that surrounded the ICP in every single place they looked to resolve their pain. In the digital and physical worlds, we led the family office space, and our pipeline was absolutely bursting.

That year, by focusing our efforts on the family office events, we literally generated tens to hundreds more high-quality opportunities compared to the massive events we previously spent hundreds of thousands of dollars on for a much smaller yield.

When you think about it, it makes sense that our dollars went much further and that we could dominate over even larger companies.

Take this simpler example with theoretical numbers. Imagine you are a medium-sized business competing against a much bigger company to sell accounting software to every business in your town. There are a thousand businesses in total. The big company has a $200,000 budget, and you have a $100,000 budget. If you each target every single business, they are spending $200 per business, and you are spending $100 per business. They are getting out twice as many messages as you and will likely be the clear winner.

Realizing you're going to lose if you go this route, you shift your approach. You recognize your product is uniquely suited to the accounting needs of gyms. There are ten gyms in town. You decide to focus your $100,000 budget exclusively on those gyms (your ICP). Now, you can spend $10,000 per gym compared to the bigger business's $200. For those gyms, you can bombard their digital space with your messaging. You can attend all their events and get involved with their insider networks. With these gyms, you have fifty times the impact compared to the giant company and their "dumb dollars," even though they had twice the budget.

Rather than being the clear loser, targeting a micro-vertical has created a context in which you can radically dominate and even beat out the giants. The secret was being obsessively focused rather than trying to send a bland message to the whole world, targeting everyone and appealing to no one.

The former strategy is precisely what we did at Sage. The mid-market in the US has around 2.4 million companies (depending on how you calculate it). The family office space has roughly 10,000 firms. Rather than spread our dollars thin and lose out to more prominent companies, we made our dollars count. Every dollar we spent targeting the family office segment was worth roughly 240 "dumb dollars" targeting anyone with a pulse. (In reality, the ratio was even steeper since we did not target all 10,000—only the ones ready to switch from their legacy systems.)

BUILD YOUR WALL OF SOUND.

Constructing a Wall of Sound

However large or limited your marketing budget is, the previous steps have equipped you to create your wall of sound for your micro-vertical of choice.

Let's unpack this wall of sound concept a bit further. An essential element of why the wall of sound works comes back to the very definition of a micro-vertical. A micro-vertical is a grouping of very similar customers with similar buyers and similar business problems. Naturally, they network and communicate with one another through specific channels. They have rankings measured by industry metrics. They gather at associations and conferences to "nerd out" at a hyper-niche level that sounds like they are speaking in code.

A perfect market is not perfect if you cannot access what can almost be considered a secret society. The networks, rankings, conferences, and associations represent the secret society that most competitors will not even be aware of. Access to these is a critical part of the perfect storm that can give you total market leadership in months.

These are the principles of creating a wall of sound:
- Focus on the ICP and the ICP buying team alone.
- Everywhere they go digitally, be there.
- Everywhere they gather physically, be there.
- Don't just sell to their community; be *part* of their community.
- Educate their community about key issues you have perspective on.
- Gather customer stories to put toward fresh messaging.
- Understand the micro-vertical better than anyone else.

Taking this approach, every dollar you spend to create demand can be hundreds of times more effective. When you have a prospect, your win rate will typically be at least three times better.

The Wall of Sound Campaign Calendar

Creating a Wall of Sound Campaign plan is a two-pronged endeavor. The first is to use ChatGPT (in addition to your understanding and connections) to gather a list of all your ICP's most essential organizations, associations, conferences, information networks, magazines, blogs, etc. The second step is to create a calendar, planning the order in which you will launch your attacks. To complete the calendar, you will need four elements:

1. **Quarterly themes**

    The quarterly themes should be the discontinuity/discontinuities. In the case of our ongoing family office example, the Smart Conversation in Chapter Five gave me four discontinuities my ICP is facing: 1) regulatory and tax pressures, 2) shift to the cloud, 3) rising complexity of family office investments, and 4) increasing demand for transparency. I would plug in those four as the quarterly themes.

    You can adapt this to whatever number of discontinuities you have found for the micro-vertical. If I only had one discontinuity, I would focus on four angles of the discontinuity as the quarterly themes. Regardless of the number of discontinuities, the output from Chapter Five makes this element simple.

2. **Monthly themes**

    Each monthly theme presents a particular angle of the quarterly theme or discontinuity. For example, let's say my quarterly theme was discontinuity #2: legacy systems are being phased out, forcing family offices to modernize with the cloud.

    For monthly themes, I would look back at the Chapter Five conversation, especially the "impact of inaction" and "reasons to do now" responses. I could make each of these my monthly themes for that quarter. Again, the Smart

Conversation history makes this calendar easy to plug and play.[19]

3. **Channels of communication**

Next, you will need a set of avenues to reach your audience. Examples include webinars, email campaigns, third-party programs, blog posts, events, Pay-Per-Lead, Pay-Per-Click, public relations, social posts, as well as analysts and association meetings. You can also think outside the box, like in the previous story, where we attended and sponsored a charity event our micro-vertical was connected with. These will form your calendar's leftmost column. You can fill this column with whatever components best suit you and your micro-vertical.

For the family office example, I would fill this column with lists of key family office associations, blogs, magazines, etc. One may already be aware of some of these from the previous research, but the Smart Conversation will help us fill this column in further.

4. **Tailored messages**

Your tailored messages will be at the heart of your calendar. These will be aligned under the quarterly and monthly themes and adapted to each specific channel of communication. While once time-consuming, this can now be done very quickly, as we saw in the previous chapter. ChatGPT can rapidly generate new messages associated with the discontinuity in the format you need.

For example, if my quarterly theme for family offices was the shift from legacy systems to the cloud, and my monthly theme was how this leads to poor financial visibility for investments, my message could be about how our product is entirely cloud-based, has bank-level security, and integrates seamlessly with their other platforms (all the pain points that might motivate them to switch!).

---

[19] For each theme or month, you can feature a key customer who has overcome the screaming pain of the discontinuity with your product or service.

Depending on the communication channel, I could adapt this into a one-line social media post or a five-hundred-word blog post.

Plus, the message does not need to be unique for every square. A colleague once compared a great message to a Thanksgiving turkey. It's not just good on the day of. Carve up those slices, and they can be adapted to any meal you like! Similarly, a great message can be written as a blog, reformatted for a LinkedIn post, restructured into a webinar, and condensed into a social media post. Reuse and recycle to make your life easier *and* keep your messaging consistent while you reach people across various mediums.

These elements form a relatively straightforward calendar like the first two-page image shown on pages 172 and 173.

The second two-page image, on pages 174 and 175, is an example of what the calendar would look like if we filled in some of the themes and messages we discovered through Smart Conversations in this book via our ongoing Sage example.

	JAN	FEB	MAR	APR	MAY	JUNE
Disconti-nuities	Major Theme for Quarter			Major Theme for Quarter		
Cage match messaging	Theme for Month	Theme for Month	Theme for Month	Theme for Month	Theme for Month	Theme for Month
Website content						
Webinars						
Emails						
3rd Party Programs						
Blogs						
Events						
PPL						
6Sense						
Social						
Analyst						
Association						

JULY	AUG	SEPT	OCT	NOV	DEC
Major Theme for Quarter			Major Theme for Quarter		
Theme for Month	Theme for Month	Theme for Month	Theme for Month	Theme for Month	Theme for Month

	JAN	FEB	MAR	APR	MAY	JUNE
Disconti-nuities	Regulatory & tax pressures			Failure of legacy systems		
Cage match messaging						
(Insert turkey slices below)						
Website content						
Webinars[20]						
Emails						
3rd Party Programs						
Blogs						
Events						
PPL						
6Sense						
Social						
Analyst						
Association						

---

[20] If I had multiple webinars or events in a month, and they were tailored to the same audience, I would likely leave them in the same row. If they were to different audiences and I needed to change the messaging, I would separate them

174

JULY	AUG	SEPT	OCT	NOV	DEC
Rising complexity of investments			Increasing demand for transparency		
Real-time multi-entity consolidation	Reduce consolidation time	Save $2mill in costs			
(Insert turkey slices below)					

into different rows. The same goes for other types of channels like events, magazines, etc.

The simple calendar forms a big picture blueprint for you to see your battle plan—how your messages are building on one another and how you are consistently spreading out your efforts. For example, you do not want all your battles to occur in Q4. Also, you want to see coordination across each different channel for the themes of the quarter. Having everything on one page makes this simple to see. And if you are working with a partner, this is your shared contract for deliverables with timelines.

The Wall of Sound Campaign: Manual Versus ChatGPT

A typical marketing calendar, while simple in design, can become overwhelming. It's often full of super expensive events that everyone believes you "*must* do" (says who?) and super costly analyst subscriptions everyone thinks you "must have" (but why?). The messages, often trying to capture a huge horizontal audience, are bland and unrelatable, not to mention laborious to create. The resulting pipeline is weak with very few resulting customers.

I remember these pains well. One time, I attended a massive show that cost hundreds of thousands of dollars for my company. The show was flashy, enormous, and prestigious. Yet *none* of our ideal customers attended. As a result, it generated no business for us. There went hundreds of thousands of dollars down the drain. After seeing these results, you'd think everyone would realize that going to that show was a waste of our time and money. Yet during the annual planning cycle meetings, people would continue to say, "We *must* do that show." In reality, a much smaller $5,000 show from our ICP's secret society generated dramatically more business and for a fraction of the cost.

When filling calendars manually, marketing and sales teams get lost in tradition, flounder in generalities, and labor over messages that don't land. No wonder the process is tedious.

The ChatGPT native, on the other hand, still has access to that available-24/7 Customer Board. The advisory board can make educated recommendations on where to allocate those marketing dollars. It can give us lists of events, associations, analysts, keywords, and customer stories, as well as which customers are already members of the associations we want to be featured by.

And of course, the speed continues to be remarkable. When pursuing family offices with Intacct in 2016, it took us a year of research to find two family office associations. In under a minute, I discovered multiple more with the following conversation.

The ChatGPT Smart Conversation: The Wall of Sound Campaign Plan

Once again, here's a quick reminder of our conversations up to this point:

- I am chatting as a marketing leader searching for growth opportunities for Sage's product, Sage Intacct.
- ChatGPT helped me identify that family offices were a cluster of our customers I could further target.
- As a family office expert, ChatGPT helped me create an ICP, identify discontinuities, and understand the competitive landscape.
- ChatGPT helped summarize my strengths and competitive advantages in a positioning statement.
- In the most recent chapter, ChatGPT adapted my positioning statement into numerous powerful messages based on my requested formats.

Continuing our Smart Conversation, we will ask ChatGPT to reveal the secret societies where our ICP hangs out, takes cues, and exchanges information. These will help us fill out the left column of our calendar and aim our messages with stealth and precision.

PROMPT 0

Me: You are an expert on the family office space, having been a Chief Investment Officer for twenty years at a well-known family office.

I am switching ChatGPT's persona back to being a family office insider. This is very important, as I want it to reveal insider communication channels that only someone deep in the family office industry would know.

Physical Networks

PROMPT 1

Me: What are the top three major associations for family offices?

ChatGPT: Family offices, which manage the investments and affairs of wealthy families, have several major associations that provide resources, networking opportunities, and advocacy. Some of the most prominent family office associations include:

- **Family Office Exchange (FOX)**
  - One of the largest and most established family office networks globally, offering resources, best practices, and a collaborative network for family offices.
- **Family Office Club**
  - A large association dedicated to connecting family offices, hosting numerous events, and providing a platform for networking and deal flow.

- **The Family Wealth Alliance**
  - o Focuses on providing family offices and wealth advisors with industry insights, best practices, and a network of peers and service providers.

These associations are the secret societies, helping family offices stay informed about industry trends, connect with peers, and access resources that support their operations and investment strategies.

PROMPT 2

Me: What are the key magazines, blogs, and events for members of the family office space?

ChatGPT: Engaging with the family office community through reputable publications, insightful blogs, and key events is essential for staying informed and connected. Here are some notable resources:

Magazines:
- **Family Office Magazine:** A leading publication offering premium content from experts in wealth management, private banking, and related sectors. It provides insights into family office trends, governance, and investment strategies.

Blogs:
- **Family Office Hub Blog:** Delivers the latest news on single and multi-family offices, their investment focuses, and industry trends, particularly in Europe.

- **Family Office Exchange (FOX) Blog:** Offers timely insights from FOX experts, members, and industry authorities on various topics relevant to family offices.

Events:

- **FAMCON—Family Office Conference:** Hosted by Family Office Magazine, this annual conference features world-leading experts discussing topics such as family office best practices, trends, governance, and alternative investments.
- **FOX Family Forum:** Organized by the Family Office Exchange, this forum brings together family members, office executives, and advisors to discuss building and strengthening lasting family enterprises.
- **ALIGN—Connecting the Family Office and the Family:** Presented by Family Business Magazine, this conference focuses on issues of governance, succession, family dynamics, and wealth & legacy management.

These resources provide valuable information and networking opportunities for professionals in the family office space, helping them stay abreast of industry developments and best practices.

Digital Networks

PROMPT 3

Me: You are an expert on Search Engine Optimization for the family office space.

PROMPT 4

Me: I am researching SEO keywords for Sage Intacct. We sell to Chief Financial Officers, Chief Investment Officers, and accountants working at a family office. What are the high-volume keywords with low competition relevant to our products and target audience?

ChatGPT: Identifying high-volume, low-competition keywords tailored to Sage Intacct's offerings for family offices is crucial for effective SEO. Here are some targeted keywords that align with your product and audience:

- **Family Office Accounting Software**
  This keyword directly addresses the software needs of family offices, highlighting solutions tailored for their accounting requirement.

- **Cloud Financial Management for Family Offices-**
  Emphasizes cloud-based financial management solutions specifically designed for family offices, aligning with Sage Intacct's offerings.

- **Investment Accounting Software for Family Offices**
  Targets family offices seeking software to manage their investment accounting, a key function for Chief Investment Officers.

- **Family Office Financial Reporting Tools**
  Focuses on tools that aid in financial reporting within family offices, appealing to CFOs and accountants.

- **Multi-Entity Accounting Solutions**
  Addresses the need for accounting solutions that handle multiple entities, common in family office structures.

- **Wealth Management Software for Family Offices**
  Highlights software solutions that assist in managing family wealth, relevant to your target audience.

- **Private Investment Office Accounting Software**
  Caters to private investment offices, often synonymous with family offices, seeking specialized accounting software.

- **Consolidated Financial Reporting for Family Offices**
  Targets the need for consolidated reporting across various family entities, a critical feature for family office accountants.

These keywords are crafted to match the specific needs and search behaviors of your target audience, enhancing the likelihood of attracting qualified leads.

Recommendations:
- **Content Development:** Create informative content around these keywords, such as blog posts, case studies, and whitepapers, to attract organic traffic.
- **On-Page Optimization:** Incorporate these keywords naturally into your website's meta titles, descriptions, headers, and body content to improve search engine rankings.
- **Competitor Analysis:** Regularly assess competitors' keyword strategies to identify new opportunities and adjust your approach accordingly.

By focusing on these targeted keywords, you can enhance Sage Intacct's visibility among family offices and their key financial decision makers.

Conversation Highlights

Previously, my team and I spent five years researching the family office space for Sage Intacct. Naturally, I recognized some of the networks ChatGPT responded with. But I did not recognize them all. Within five minutes, ChatGPT found associations, magazines, blogs, and events I had not seen in my five years of researching and interacting with the family office space.

I told you: these niche communities are like secret societies; if you aren't part of them, it's arduous to tap into their networks. ChatGPT helped us discover even more of these secret networks we could tap into. Lastly, the keyword question provided a great starting point for content writers trying to speak to these secret societies and reel them toward us.

Key Output for Step 7

With these questions and even more that you can add, you have everything you need to fill in your Wall of Sound Campaign Calendar:

- A Wall of Sound Campaign Calendar template
- Discontinuities and "risks of inaction" from Chapter Five (to fill in quarterly and monthly themes)
- A list of gatherings and insider communication channels to reach your micro-vertical (to go in the left column of your calendar)
- A strategy for hitting your audience with wave after wave of your messaging through all their most valued insider channels

How to Advocate for This Approach

At this stage, you've seen the evidence that this method works. However, if you are part of a marketing or sales team, you may not have the authority to reorient your team under this mission.

Unfortunately, many people—*especially* executives who have been doing this a long time—hold deeply-entrenched opinions to support a horizontal strategy. If you advocate for this approach, you will likely encounter the arguments of "The product is horizontal" and/or "We can't afford to make our product more vertically specific."

To advocate for this approach more effectively, I recommend running a trial to see what this method can do for your team and comparing it with the existing approach. With the help of generative AI, this trial will not take you all that long. Present the results to your team. It's easy to argue with ideas; it's difficult to argue with a great plan.

CHAPTER 10
Measuring Success & Looking Ahead

Let us end where we started: in the marketer's war room. You have plotted out the hills you wanted to win, built out your strategy, and now you are on the hills sharing your message with the residents. Hopefully, they are now running into your arms, seeing you as the liberator from the tyranny of legacy systems.

Results on the ground may seem positive, but the general (or Settlers of Catan aficionado) will want to look back at the big picture and ask: who has the most territory? Did we win the hills we set out for? Was the campaign successful? And where shall we go next?

Entire books could be and have been written on each of these subjects. I have also given numerous presentations on these topics. These topics are too big to be covered comprehensively in the scope of this book. For our purposes here, I will give a simplified overview of measuring success and predicting the future using the Smart Conversation approach we have established. My aim is to set you up for further exploration and experimentation.

Becoming A Market Leader

In the early 2000s, I became the CMO of the software company Alfresco. As mentioned in the messaging chapter, I joined Alfresco when it was very new with a small team of twelve.

In the shadow of high-end enterprise players, no one knew who we were. One early customer told us, "It's lucky I found you guys. When I search for Alfresco, all that comes up is outdoor dining sets and barbeques." Indeed, when we checked our search engine ranking, we were buried pages beneath outdoor (or "alfresco") dining furniture and accoutrements.

We went to work focusing on content writing, blogging, distribution, and executing our micro-vertical campaign strategy. We found our market and began seeing hordes of users longing for a service like ours that sat between the super expensive enterprise option and the low-quality bundled programs.

About a year later, we rechecked our search engine results. This time, we were not just outranking outdoor dining sets (which is harder than you'd think!). We were also outranking all of our other billion-dollar competitors *combined*.

The signs of success were many: We had become the most searched-for content management platform. The number of people downloading our open-source product skyrocketed. The number of users opting for our paid account also dramatically increased. We were also ranked as the winner on one of the most broadly referenced software comparison directories.

We knew we had won the hill we set out for. Alfresco soon became the world's most valuable private open-source company (at the time) and a clear leader in the space.

Markers of Market Leadership

What we achieved at Alfresco is the goal of the Smart Conversations method in this book—that you would win enough territory to become a superpower in your chosen space. This is otherwise known as **market leadership**, which refers to the degree of influence a company holds over a particular market.

There are many markers one can use to gauge market leadership. Here are some common indicators that you have become the market leader:

- The leading companies have chosen you as their provider.
- Your customers love you.
- The related service providers want to partner with you as their first choice.

- Your primary competitor doesn't even bother to compete for your hill.
- When people write about this micro-vertical, they consistently mention you.
- You have significant market share.[21]

Examples of market leaders in the Internet age are easy to see, like Apple, Google, Amazon, and Microsoft within information technology. Boeing and Caterpillar are market leaders in capital goods; Salesforce for SaaS based CRM; Costco and Walmart for consumer staples; Air BnB and American Tower for real estate.

Each industry will have its own more specific markers to indicate whether it is leading and by how much. Criteria for SaaS market leadership include factors like innovation and category creation, ecosystem and platform stickiness, and M&A (merger and acquisition) expanding markets. These are very different from how supermarkets might measure market leadership—with criteria like the number of shoppers with loyalty cards, gross revenue, and revenue per square foot. Documentum achieved market leader status when we became the corporate standard within the pharmaceutical R&D industry within eighteen months. It's extremely rare to take over a market of this size so quickly. We became such a standard that even the FDA accepted new drug applications directly into Documentum.

Like I said, the criteria for leadership in each industry will be different, but once you become a leader, you'll know.

Measuring Leadership: The Joining of AI and Gen AI

With this book's strategy building up to the Wall of Sound Campaign, one can achieve market leadership in as little as twelve to

---

[21] It's difficult to put numbers to this because most companies are private and do not publicize how much market share they have. In the enterprise space, a company with more than 30% market share is often considered a market leader. However, in the open source space, market leadership can require as much as 80% market share. It varies by industry.

eighteen months (when you focus on the right type of hill). That said, you don't need to wait until the campaign ends to tell if it is going successfully. Great generals know how to evaluate mid-battle.

The manual way to evaluate mid-battle would be through funnel analysis: seeing how many high-quality opportunities we're getting, how big they are on average, how quickly they're closing, and where the best leads are coming from. In the last decade, AI-powered systems like Salesforce and 6Sense have developed to give teams much more useful insight into this data and the patterns it reveals. Any team doing funnel analysis without one of these AI systems would unarguably benefit from switching over.

That said, Smart Conversations are highly complementary to these existing tools. This is the meeting of AI and Gen AI. The AI tools can give you insight into an individual prospect's *intent* and how likely they are to buy. This is extremely valuable on its own, but a Smart Conversation fills out the big picture with more color. From ChatGPT, we can learn: Is there a market leader? What makes someone a market leader? How am I doing? And what can I do to get better?

Not to mention, the AI systems provide insight on individual accounts, but the method in this book helps you target and win a whole *group* of accounts rather than going one by one. (The traditional term for what AI systems do is Account-Based Marketing, or ABM. I call this system **Account-Based Micro-Vertical Marketing**, or **ABMM**.) ABMM builds on the strengths of the intent scoring system while expanding its potential reach and scale.

Combining these tools provides incredible insight into how you are doing with both individual accounts and the micro-vertical.

Planning Your Next Move

Of course, measuring success goes hand-in-hand with planning your next steps.

If you survey the battle and see that you are still falling behind, you likely need to go back and adjust your plan. You may have missed a red flag with your micro-vertical and should have qualified it out sooner. You may have misunderstood the discontinuity, perhaps your product does not truly address the discontinuity, or there may be no discontinuity after all. It's possible you miscalculated your competitor's approach or made one of the common mistakes described in the chapters on positioning and messaging.

Sometimes, it takes a few tries to calibrate your approach. Don't be afraid to start over on your strategy, go back to interviews, or pivot to a new micro-vertical. Remember: This playbook makes you nimble, able to keep up with an ever-changing battlefield. With this method, redoing a plan takes a day, not three months. Use that to your advantage.

On the other hand, if you survey the battle and see that you are winning, congratulations! First things first: Stay the course. Don't change the plan or the messaging just because you've been staring at it for so long that you get bored with it. Of course, keep your eyes and ears open for new trends, needs, or competitors you may need to accommodate. But if the plan activates your target audience and drives them to you, keep at it and see it through.

Second, like any ambitious general, you'll probably start eyeing what hill you can take over next. My colleague Peyton says we are "taking over the world one micro-vertical at a time."

My colleague's sentiment is not just ambitious—it is true. You may have crafted a message for a very specific audience, but there is always a bigger audience for a great message. There are plenty who have yet to hear it.

There is always a bigger audience for a great message.

The micro-vertical hills strategy perfectly sets you up to expand your territory into adjacent hills that are similar to your micro-vertical and likely share some networks and connections. You'll have to adapt your plan, but only slightly compared to finding a whole new audience.

CLAIMED GROUND-AND NEARBY PEAKS READY TO BE WON

The ChatGPT Smart Conversation: Measuring Success and Looking Ahead

This is our final Smart Conversation of the book. In it, we assume that I, a marketing person for Sage, have completed all the previous steps in this book. ChatGPT helped me identify my cluster, ICP, discontinuities, and competition. Based on all this, it has helped me craft a positioning statement and messaging to target my micro-vertical of family offices through a Wall of Sound Campaign.

Now, we are assuming I have begun the Wall of Sound Campaign and am using a Smart Conversation to see how I am doing with the hill so far—and if I am successful, where I might consider expanding next. Let's begin.

PROMPT 0

Me: You are a SaaS analytics expert.

PROMPT 1

Me: What are the indicators of market leadership for SaaS accounting software companies in the family office space?

ChatGPT: Market leadership in the family office segment of SaaS accounting is not solely based on revenue or market share. It's defined by how well a platform meets the unique, high-stakes needs of ultra-high-net-worth (UHNW) families and their advisors. This summary outlines the top indicators of market leadership in this space and how Sage stands out.

Depth in Multi-Entity & Partnership Accounting
- **Why It Matters:** Family offices manage dozens or hundreds of entities—trusts, LLCs, foundations, and partnerships—across jurisdictions.

- **Leadership Signals:**
  - Automated multi-entity consolidation and inter-company eliminations
  - Capital accounts, carried interest, and waterfall calculations
  - Multi-currency functionality with real-time reporting

Seamless Integration with Investment Platforms

- **Why It Matters:** Family offices require accurate performance tracking across private equity, hedge funds, and traditional investments.
- **Leadership Signals:**
  - Pre-built or open API integrations with platforms like Addepar, Black Diamond, FundCount
  - Live NAV, IRR, and investment allocation reporting

Trust & Security for UHNW Families

- **Why It Matters:** Security, privacy, and auditability are non-negotiable in wealth management
- **Leadership Signals:**
  - SOC 2, ISO 27001, MFA, encryption in transit and at rest
  - Role-based access and audit trails
  - Permission structures aligned with family hierarchy

Nonprofit & Philanthropy Management

- **Why It Matters:** Many family offices manage donor-advised funds (DAFs), foundations, and grant programs.
- **Leadership Signals:**
  - Fund accounting, 990 tracking, and encumbrance reporting
  - Philanthropy dashboards and donor rollups

Vendor Credibility & Segment Penetration

- **Why It Matters:** Family offices rely on peer validation and discretion. Public endorsements are rare.
- **Leadership Signals:**
  - Referenceable client base within family office networks
  - Analyst recognition specific to UHNW and wealth tech (not just broad ERP reports)

Low IT Overhead with High Configurability

- **Why It Matters:** Family offices don't want to operate like enterprises. They need powerful tech without the overhead.
- **Leadership Signals:**
  - Cloud-native architecture with low-code customization
  - Fast deployment and business-user configurability

Support for Generational Wealth Transition & Governance

- **Why It Matters:** Next-gen family members expect transparency, mobility, and digital-native workflows.
- **Leadership Signals:**
  - Custom dashboards for heirs, trustees, and external advisors
  - Mobile access, ESG/impact reporting, and governance workflows

PROMPT 2

Me: Based on these, how strong is Sage Intacct's market leadership in the family office space?

ChatGPT: Sage Intacct shows strong leadership in multiple dimensions of family office financial management. Here's how it aligns to the seven indicators of market leadership:

Market Leadership Indicator	Sage Intacct's Performance
Multi-Entity & Consolidation	Best-in-class automation, real-time rollups across 100+ entities
Investment Integration	Integrates with Addepar, Black Diamond, FundCount via open APIs
Security & Compliance	SOC 2 certified, granular permissions, audit trails
Nonprofit Support	Strong foundation features: fund accounting, grant tracking, 990s
Brand Reputation	Growing, not yet dominant vs. legacy systems like Geneva/Investran
Cloud Agility	Cloud-native, deploys in weeks, highly configurable
Governance Tools	Dashboards for stakeholders, ESG-friendly features

Overall, Sage Intacct is a top performer for family offices managing $100M–$2B AUM and 5–50 entities—especially those seeking modern, scalable, and secure financial platforms.

Final Assessment & Market Position
- **Where Sage Intacct Leads:**
  - Mid-sized single & multi-family offices with growing complexity
  - Multi-entity, multi-currency accounting and audit automation
  - Nonprofit and foundation support built natively into the platform
  - Real-time visibility and integration with wealth systems
- **Limitations**
  - Not a native investment management platform—requires external tools for NAV and portfolio analytics

o Less brand penetration among UHNW firms ($2B+ AUM) compared to legacy vendors

- **Leadership Scorecard (1–5 Scale)**

Category	Score	Comments
Multi-Entity Accounting	5/5	Industry-leading automation and scalability
Investment Integration	4/5	Strong APIs, but not native tracking
Security & Compliance	4/5	SOC 2, robust controls
Nonprofit Capabilities	5/5	Ideal for family foundations and DAFs
Brand & Ecosystem Reach	3/5	Growing, but not top of mind in UHNW circles
Deployment & Agility	5/5	Fast rollout, low-code config
Next-Gen Transparency	4/5	Strong dashboards, ESG support

Conclusion:

Sage is a market leader for modernizing the financial back-office of family offices in the mid-market. Its strengths in multi-entity accounting, nonprofit support, cloud agility, and governance tools make it a clear choice for firms transitioning away from legacy systems.

With strategic focus and deeper investment integrations, it can become the dominant SaaS financials player in the family office space.

Assuming we were not the market leader before implementing the Wall of Sound Campaign, the response above demonstrated significant progress. You could ask ChatGPT this same question periodically throughout your campaign rollout (say, every three months) to watch your market leadership "report card" go up.

I was going to ask about our limitations and how we could grow in market leadership, but it already included this in its response to my previous question. To probe this further for your purposes, you can ask it about your limitations more explicitly with follow-up questions.

PROMPT 3
Me: Based on Sage Intacct's success with family offices, what adjacent markets could Sage target?

ChatGPT: Sage Next Growth Opportunity: Expansion into Adjacent Markets

Ideal Adjacent Market – Registered Investment Advisors (RIAs)

- **Why RIAs Are a Strategic Fit**
  - Sage Intacct's success in the family office segment positions it well to serve Registered Investment Advisors (RIAs)—a market with overlapping needs:

Shared Need	Family Offices	RIAs
Multi-Entity Accounting	Core functionality	Core functionality
SEC/FINRA Compliance	High relevance	High relevance
Integration with Wealth Platforms	Addepar, Black Diamond	Orion, Tamarac, Addepar
Performance-Based Revenue Tracking	Sometimes present	Mission-critical
Audit Trails & Role-Based Access	Required	Required

- **Sage Intacct Advantages**
  - Native multi-entity & partnership accounting with consolidation
  - Open API architecture enables quick integration with RIA tech stacks
  - Audit-ready reporting satisfies compliance reviews and client transparency expectations
  - Cloud-based, fast to deploy, and low IT overhead—ideal for lean RIA ops
- **Strategic Opportunity:** Position Sage Intacct as the "financial system of record for RIAs"—just as it is for family offices—focusing on those managing $500M–$5B AUM with complex entity needs.

Additional Markets for Expansion

Market	Opportunity	Why It Aligns with Sage Intacct
Private Equity & Venture Capital Firms	Automate fund accounting & waterfalls	Similar to family office investment structures
Foundations & Endowments	Expand nonprofit capabilities	Leverage existing strengths in fund/grant accounting
Multi-Generational Trust Companies	Complex family entity management	Hybrid between RIAs & family offices

- **Strategic Shift: From Family Office to Wealth Infrastructure**
  o Sage Intacct can evolve from:
    "The financial engine for family offices" into "The financial platform for modern wealth management firms"
- **This Allows Entry Into:**
  o RIAs seeking operational scale and audit readiness
  o PE/VC firms needing visibility across funds
  o Foundations modernizing their financial reporting
- **Key Next Steps:**
  o Develop RIA-specific ICPs and GTM campaigns
  o Build deeper investment platform integrations (Orion, Tamarac, etc.)
  o Partner with RIA-focused consultants and system integrators

Summary:
RIAs represent a natural next market, with shared requirements around compliance, transparency, and multi-entity structures. With its proven success in family offices, Sage is well-positioned to expand into a broader wealth tech leadership role.

Conversation Highlights

In this Smart Conversation, ChatGPT demonstrated a deep knowledge of market leadership for our specific type of company in the specific area of our micro-vertical. I didn't feed it any other data or insights, and it discerned both our areas of leadership and our limitations. It even gave us a report card with clear areas we can focus on to expand our leadership ranking.

The question about adjacent markets is meant to discern which hills we should target next. The response about expansion especially wowed me. I have spent most of my career in this space. I was expecting it to say that we could expand into venture capital firms, which we have already done. But the other three options took me by surprise. I had never seriously considered those before or realized the opportunity there with such clarity.

I anticipate you will find the same: a deeper understanding of market leadership, how close you are to winning the battle, and where you can expand. One could even run these questions periodically throughout the Wall of Sound Campaign to watch ChatGPT's response change. It's gratifying to watch your report card score go up.

Key Output from Step 8

By the end of this step, you now have the following:

- The criteria of market leadership for your specific micro-vertical
- How close you are to market leadership and how you can still grow
- Adjacent micro-verticals or "hills" you're positioned to target next

Conclusion

When I started researching and experimenting for this book, I wanted to see if generative AI was as big a change for business strategy planning as the Internet was. Put simply, it is. Generative AI has changed the typical business strategy playbook for every CEO, CMO, CRO, investor, and team member. I will never write, coach, or review a business strategy plan without a generative AI application next to me again.

As marketing and sales professionals and business owners, we must recognize the discontinuity we are facing in our own courts. Sure, the old ways may be working fine now. But I do believe this discontinuity will determine how we survive into the future.

With the use of these tools, we have the power to engage and energize our audience members like never before. There is nothing like seeing a target customer transform into your biggest fan and advocate. The momentum is palpable as you stand atop the conquered hill, knowing you can do it all over again.

To this point, I would like to reintroduce the quote from the Harvard Business Review on how people are using Gen AI: "People who don't find it useful simply haven't really understood how to use it. The 5% or whatever who use it effectively are going to smoke the others."

Like I said, this book is about making you part of that 5%. The percentage who understands that generative AI is not just a way to "super search" or automate the old ways of doing things. This subset of people (now including you) is equipped to go beyond simplistic prompts into full-blown Smart Conversations, opening up immeasurable possibilities for anything your business needs.

Of course, the technology at the center of this book will continue evolving. But the principles of how to interact with it—and how not to underestimate it—will serve us all as we continue to engage with generative AI in ways we never thought possible.

Armed with the Gen AI-first mindset, you can rapidly win hill after hill, targeting prospects down to the tribe level while sweeping across the map.

Welcome to the new world. Welcome to the 5%.

Conversation Library

Below, I've compiled the principles of Smart Conversations, as well as all the prompts and key outputs in the book. This section is ideal for readers who don't have time to read the whole book or who want an easy way to find the conversations as they implement this strategy in their own work.

I recommend using this library as a conversational guideline rather than a rigid list. Like any good recipe, it invites you to add your own flavors and adjust it to your liking. You'll swap your own details for the Sage-specific questions. In addition, I encourage you to make the conversation your own and ask follow-up questions that will help you get the most out of this tool. After all, that's what makes it a *conversation*: It is fluid, dynamic, and adaptable. Enjoy the exploration.

Principles of Smart Conversations

At a high level, these are the principles for conducting Smart Conversations. You can review these in greater detail at the end of Chapter One.

- Give ChatGPT a persona.
- Be specific.
- Ask one question at a time.
- Input customer data.
- Utilize ChatGPT's workspace (which is called a GPT).
- Use ChatGPT's access to the Internet.
- Remember that ChatGPT has memory.
- Ask follow-up questions.

Chapter 3
The ChatGPT Smart Conversation:
Cluster Analysis

Upload:
A spreadsheet containing your customer names, websites, and respective industry labels (exported from your CRM).

Prompts:
- You are an industry marketing expert with specific experience in the segmentation of finance and insurance companies.
- How many industries are blank?
- Can you replace them with the correct industry where possible?
- Please infer where you can.
- "Finance & Insurance" and "Finance" are very broad categories. Can you analyze this category to be more specific?
- Can you break this down to the next level of granularity?
- Can you add a column that shows the next level of granularity and name the column "industry drilldown"?
- Can you add a column with NAICS codes?
- Can you analyze NAICS codes, do a count by category, and display a graph?
- I have attached a publicly available list of family offices. Based on the website column, how many are in both spreadsheets?
- Can you update the spreadsheet to say "family office" for the 49 that appear?
- Can you do a count by industry?

Key Output from Step 1:

- A list of both major and minor clusters (micro-verticals) within your existing customer base—with a complete audit trail of how you got them
- For each cluster, an industry identification and ranking
- Identification of the biggest and potentially most valuable clusters

Chapter 4
The ChatGPT Smart Conversation: Developing the Ideal Customer Profile

Upload:

- Transcripts of any manual interviews you've done
- PDF LinkedIn Profiles of 7–10 decision makers in the market you want to target
- Optional: any public bios, customer posts, interview articles, case studies, public presentations, or company reports that might give further insight into the ideal customer

Prompts:

- You are an expert at developing industry marketing plans for the family offices market after having worked in that space for 20 years.
- I need to create an Ideal Customer Profile for the buying team based on the attached customer profiles. Browse the web and find any family office public case studies, press articles on family office customers, blogs on family office customers, or other family office customer reference materials from third parties. Do you have enough information to complete the task?

- Can you expand on the buying team? Specifically, their role, influence in the buying process, major pains, requirements, and background?

Key Output from Step 2:

- An ICP representing companies in the micro-vertical you want to target
- A customer persona for each member of the ICP's buying team
- A rational idea of whether you should
  - Pursue: Your product/service fits the ICP's needs in this micro-vertical.
  - Pause: Do further research to see if this micro-vertical is a fit for you.
  - Pivot: Your product/service does not fit the ICP's needs; you have qualified out this micro-vertical and can now explore others.

Chapter 5
The ChatGPT Smart Conversation:
Discovering Discontinuities

Prompts:
- When you examine the key challenges and needs for the ICP, which ones are most compelling to address now rather than next year?
- When you look at the compelling reasons for immediate action ("do now"), what is the impact of not doing them?
- What is the discontinuity or market shift driving these "do now" pains?

Key Output from Step 3:

- A concise summary of your ICP's most significant challenges and needs
- A list of which challenges are genuine discontinuities to act on
- Further clarity on whether to:
  - ○ Pursue: Your micro-vertical has a true discontinuity and is motivated to become your customer.
  - ○ Ponder: Do further research to better understand whether there is a discontinuity and/or if you have the solution.
  - ○ Pivot: Even if you have what the customer needs, there is no motivation to make a change; you have qualified out this micro-vertical and can now explore others.

Chapter 6
The ChatGPT Smart Conversation

PART 1: Competitive Analysis

Prompts:
- Who are the legacy on-premises family office specialists in the mid-market of 20 to 999 employees that compete against the product, Sage Intacct?
- You are now an expert in the cloud financial space, having been an analyst for over 20 years.
- Can you tell me how cloud-based financial solutions address the key discontinuities in the family office space?
- Who are the top 3 major cloud financial SaaS players in the mid-market of 20 to 999 employees?
- What product is the primary competitor for Sage Intacct?

- For Sage Intacct to win against its competitors, what are the top five SaaS applications it needs, and what partners will those require?

PART 2: Finding Competitive Discontinuities

Prompts:
- Can you link the ICP pains and discontinuities to the strengths of Sage Intacct and the weaknesses of NetSuite?

Key Output for Step 4

- A list of ways your product addresses the true discontinuities of your target market
- A list and in-depth comparison of your top competitors
- A list of key metrics the competition is based on
- A side-by-side assessment of your strengths and your competitor's weaknesses in addressing the customer's discontinuities
- Further clarity on whether to:
  - Pursue: Legacy competitors will be ousted by the market shift; you are stronger than your competitor in fixing the ICP's most urgent and critical pain.
  - Ponder: You and your competitor have similar solutions to fixing the urgent pain; work to see if you can meaningfully differentiate yourself.
  - Pivot: Even if there is a true discontinuity, another new-world competitor has dominated the market first.

Chapter 7
The ChatGPT Smart Conversation: Positioning Statement

Prompts:

- You are an expert on cloud financials and messaging for the family office space.
- Based on the information you have, can you create a classic Geoffrey Moore Positioning Statement for the Sage Intacct product in the family office space?
- Can you produce an extended positioning statement for Sage Intacct in the family office space with the following structure:
  - **For**
    - Include buyer personas for each person on the buying team.
    - Include names of companies or firms that are industry leaders and lend credibility to your strength in the micro-vertical.
  - **Who need to**
    - Mention the whole industry discontinuity.
    - Mention the impact of the discontinuity.
    - State the critical need.
  - **Sage Intacct is the only** Cloud-based Financial Management System
  - **That provides**
    - Include metrics that show how you solve the critical need above in terms of the following:
      - Overall benefit
      - Specific time benefit
      - Specific cost benefit
      - Specific growth benefit
      - Specific risk benefit
      - Specific regulatory benefit

  o **Unlike**
  - Name Legacy Competitor 1 (being phased out by discontinuity).
  - Name Legacy Competitor 2 (being phased out by discontinuity).
  - Name New-World Competitor 1 and mention weaknesses like the following:
    - Not focused on this micro-vertical
    - No key customers to lend credibility
    - Lack of micro-vertical understanding
    - Lack of critical product functionality needed for this micro-vertical

Key Output for Step 5

- The one-page extended positioning statement summarizing the strategy and Go-To-Market for the micro-vertical
- A starting point to adapt if you want to target other related micro-verticals next

Chapter 8
The ChatGPT Smart Conversation: Differentiated Power Messaging

Prompts:
- Based on the positioning statement, can you create a 50-word elevator pitch demonstrating understanding of the customer, discontinuity, and competitive advantages?
- Can you create a 25-word messaging statement encompassing the single most powerful differentiator?
- Can you create a 10-word messaging statement encompassing the single most powerful differentiator?
- Can you create a tagline encompassing the single most powerful differentiator?

- Based on the extended positioning statement, can you develop messaging using the "Droid Does" campaign structure of:
  o Does your [category] do [leading differentiator A]?
  o Does your [category] do [leading differentiator B]?
  o Does your [category] do [leading differentiator C]?
  o Sage Intacct Does.
- Based on the extended positioning statement, can you develop messaging using the Metaphor messaging structure Marc Benioff used to describe Salesforce:
  "Salesforce.com is Amazon.com meets Siebel Systems."
- Based on the extended positioning statement, can you develop messaging using the Best-of-Both campaign structure: "[My product] provides the [strength] of [product A] combined with the [strength] of [product 2]?"
- You are a messaging expert in cloud accounting and family office spaces. Based on the Metaphor messaging structure, can you create eight variations for the Sage Intacct product?
- Can you create a competition to see which is the best messaging and show me the top four, two, and one?

Upload:
Ian Howells' public LinkedIn profile PDF, recent interviews, blog posts, quotes from the annual report, etc.
- What messaging would Ian Howells prefer and why?

Key Output for Step 6

- A variety of concise, compelling messages, based on the facts from the positioning statement, for contexts like the elevator pitch, website copy, PPC, ads, trade shows, and 1:1 conversations
- A way to rapidly test which messages are best
- A way to rapidly tailor these messages to any individual or context

Chapter 9
The ChatGPT Smart Conversation: The Wall of Sound Campaign Plan

Prompts:

- You are an expert on the family office space, having been a CIO for twenty years at a well-known family office.
- What are the top three major associations for family offices?
- What are the key magazines, blogs, and events for members of the family office space?
- You are an expert on Search Engine Optimization for the family office space.
- I am researching SEO keywords for Sage Intacct. We sell to Chief Financial Officers, Chief Investment Officers, and accountants working at a family office. What are the high-volume keywords with low competition relevant to our products and target audience?

Key Output for Step 7

- A Wall of Sound Campaign Calendar template
- Discontinuities and "risks of inaction" from Chapter Five (to fill in quarterly and monthly themes)
- A list of gatherings and insider communication channels to reach your micro-vertical (to go in the left column of your calendar)
- A strategy for hitting your audience with wave after wave of your messaging through all their most valued insider channels

Chapter 10
The ChatGPT Smart Conversation:
Measuring Success and Looking Ahead

Prompts:
- You are a SaaS analytics expert.
- What are the indicators of market leadership for SaaS accounting software companies in the family office space?
- Based on these, how strong is Sage's market leadership in the family office space?
- Based on Sage's success with family offices, what adjacent market could I target?

Key Output from Step 8

- By the end of this step, you now have the following:
  - The criteria of market leadership for your specific micro-vertical
  - How close you are to market leadership and how you can still grow
  - Adjacent micro-verticals or "hills" you're positioned to target next

Acknowledgements

Throughout my career, I have been lucky enough to work with exceptional people. I want to express my deepest gratitude to two people in particular: John Newton and Robert Reid. John took a chance on me fresh out of school after my PhD, and Rob was the person who made me believe in marketing. I had the privilege of working for John at three companies—Ingres, Documentum, and Alfresco—and for Rob at two—Documentum and Intacct. Initially, these men were my colleagues. Over time, they became my mentors, and for many years now, they have been great friends.

I also want to acknowledge someone who has become a personal hero. My hero is not a professional athlete or film star—it's Geoffrey A. Moore. I absorbed everything he said during my time at Documentum and have read all his work, from *Crossing the Chasm* to *The Infinite Staircase*. His wisdom has profoundly shaped both my career and this book.

Writing this book has been a long-held goal, and I sincerely appreciate those who helped me refine it from the early drafts to its final form. I offer a special thank you to my boys—Tom, Jamie, Rory, and Phil Bradley—who all work in tech. I'm also grateful to Michelle Denogean of Mindtrip for her in-depth feedback. At Sage, I'd like to thank Peyton Burch, Dom Ballinger, and Tina Wang—who have been encouraging me to write a book for years.

Writing a book is hard work; I couldn't have done it without Abby Dengler. She coached me through the ups and downs of the writing process, and she has become a good friend whom I worried about during the LA fires. Abby took the raw text and shaped it into what it is today.

I would also like to thank Carmen Berry of Berry Powell Press for continually challenging me and opening my eyes to new perspectives. Berry Powell Press is much more than a book publisher.

Their team, which includes Carolyn Rafferty, Valeri Mills Barnes, Marianne Cronquist, and Kay McConnaughey, helped me achieve a dream I could not have realized on my own.

Most importantly, I want to thank my wonderful, patient wife, Carla, who put up with me jumping out of bed at 4 a.m. whenever inspiration struck, often waking her up in the process.

Lastly, I'd like to thank Dan Miller for giving me a call. My happiest days at work have been at Intacct, led by Rob Reid, and Sage, now led by Steve Hare.

About the Author

Dr. Ian Howells is a visionary strategist and marketing pragmatist with over two decades of experience scaling B2B SaaS businesses. As the architect behind some of the most innovative go-to-market strategies in enterprise software, Ian has pioneered the fusion of micro-vertical marketing and generative AI to deliver precision, speed, and scale not previously possible.

Ian held executive roles at iconic software companies, from Silicon Valley startups like Documentum to global cloud leaders like Sage, helping build categories and craft stories that resonate across industries. In *Smart Conversations*, he distills a blueprint for the next era of B2B growth—where AI meets micro-vertical segmentation, and every message moves markets. His work empowers leaders to move beyond tactics and into intelligent, whole-system thinking.

Ian holds a PhD in Distributed Databases from Cardiff University. Learn more and connect with Ian at:

www.drianhowells.com.

Note from the Publisher
Berry Powell Press
Carmen Berry, Founder
New York Times bestselling author

Berry Powell Press was founded to bring new ideas to those seeking solutions. Ian is a visionary with a unique way of seeing the world, and we are honored to share his insights. His perspective has the power to transform the way businesses operate, helping them reach their goals with greater efficiency and precision. This book is especially timely as AI continues to reshape how we understand and engage with the world. We need deep thinkers—individuals who are willing to explore complex challenges and guide us through this evolving landscape. While many people are generalists, capable of doing a variety of things well, Ian is different. He delves deeply into specific problems, bringing the vision and discipline necessary to create groundbreaking solutions on the cutting edge of advanced technology.

As a small business owner, I particularly appreciate how this book democratizes access to AI marketing tools. Traditionally, only large corporations could afford data-driven, hyper-personalized strategies. This book helps level the playing field, enabling small businesses and startups to harness cutting-edge innovation and seize new opportunities.

Ian's intelligence is matched by his dedication to making a positive impact. At Berry Powell Press, we champion voices like his—those who use their expertise as a force for good. It is our privilege to help bring his work to the world, empowering businesses and readers alike.

We at Berry Powell Press are committed to cultivating authors and their life-changing messages through building a collaborative, creative community of authors and publishing professionals. If you have a book rumbling around inside of you that needs to be written and released, please contact us, and we can explore if we might be a fit.

Visit our website at www.berrypowellpress.com

Berry Powell Press is a hybrid publishing house that publishes authors with transformational perspectives on timely personal and societal challenges. We provide our authors with in-depth mentorship and collaborative assistance to create life-changing books. Additionally, we assist them in building book-based businesses that can impact the largest audience possible. We publish fiction and non-fiction for adults and children.

Made in the USA
Columbia, SC
17 March 2026

05fd16b9-24a9-4898-aff4-1aa942efca7aR01